Tapestries of the Heart

Emerging Poets of the 21st Century Volume 1

By

Various Authors

This book is a work of fiction. Places, events, and situations in this story are purely fictional. Any resemblance to actual persons, living or dead, is coincidental.

© 2003 by Various Authors. All rights reserved.

No part of this book may be reproduced, stored in a retrieval system, or transmitted by any means, electronic, mechanical, photocopying, recording, or otherwise, without written permission from the author.

ISBN: 1-4140-2079-1 (e-book)
ISBN: 1-4140-2077-5 (Paperback)
ISBN: 1-4140-2078-3 (Dust Jacket)

Library of Congress Control Number: 2003097920

This book is printed on acid free paper.

Printed in the United States of America
Bloomington, IN

1stBooks – rev. 12/19/03

Acknowledgement

A book may come to mind, an idea may be schemed, a thinker may be applauded for thoughts that come to life but it is the doer that makes the dream come true. To that end, I can not advance another page without acknowledging the doers in this venture that helped me bring this once nice thought to the reality you hold today. From the day I sent an email asking if they would like to make a book, James Hastings and Michael Cotner have carried the banner high. The hours and hours and countless readings, the nights spent glaring at a screen, the gnashing of teeth and the pain of choosing, all done without a whimper without a promise or a penny to claim. The eagerness Sherri Tillman displayed and the talent we discovered when she sent the magnificent cover selections to us for this book. It is with great honor we dedicate the cover to her. The illustrations in this wonderful book are by the hand of the incredible Cynthia Jeanne Rider. Volunteering to do the illustrations was a major sacrifice of time and we appreciate it more than she will ever know.

Finally, we all thank the authors that gave us their great pieces to put into this first of its kind poetry book. Obviously without their contributions this book would not be. They wrote, they gave and they did so without promise of stardom. Satisfied just to have their pieces shown to the world, they never hesitated a second.

I want to thank-you; thank you all for making this the greatest experience of my life.

Jim Furber

Introduction

Welcome to Tapestries of the Heart, Volume 1 of Emerging Poets of the Twenty-First Century. This project is the brainchild of three poets who, together, believed that the public was ready for a fresh sampling of new and very talented artists. Through much tedious yet rewarding labor of writing and re-writing, editing and re-editing, James Furber, Michael Cotner, and James Hastings present to the reader a book of unparalleled emotion and imagery. Every poem presented is destined to touch your heart.

You are about to embark into some outstanding works of verse from a sampling of the most talented and, until now, unknown poets in the world. While these artists are not household names, you will find their works to be of the highest caliber. If you are seeking something out of the mainstream of contemporary poetry, you have acquired the right book.

It is the goal of the creators of this project to bring new, aspiring poets into public circulation. However, do not expect amateurish works here for you will find none. Every poet selected has honed their art form to razor-like sharpness and their ability to create worlds with their words will astound you.

This book is divided into sections according to subject category. At the end of the book, there will be a short biography of each poet so as to familiarize you with the "soul behind the magic."

It is our sincere hope that Emerging Poets of the Twenty-first Century, Vol. 1 will be the first of many exciting books, bringing forth the new genius of a new millennium. The best to you, and happy reading!

James Hastings
Michael Cotner
James M. Furber

Dedication

This book is dedicated to the teacher, the construction worker, the shop keeper, nurse, and the housewife. All of whom share a common love of writing and hold dear a life long dream of having their heartfelt work recognized in a professional, widely publicized forum. These undiscovered, yet extremely talented "word masters" are everywhere; you might even be married to one. May this book be a beacon of hope that the dream is reachable.

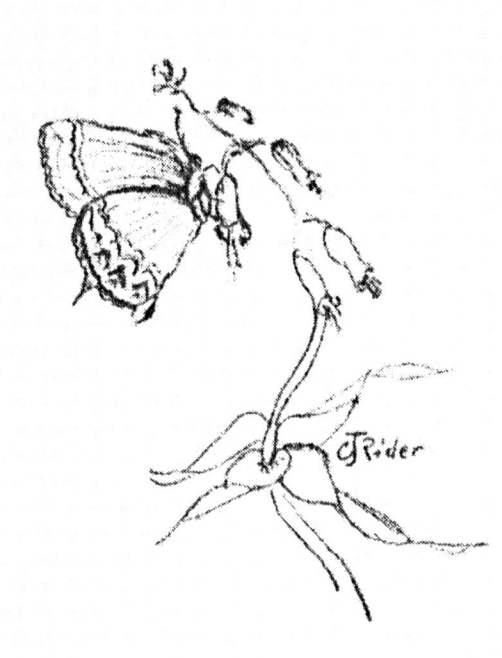

C.J. Rider

Table of Contents

Acknowledgement iii

Introduction v

Dedication vii

   Publisher's Choice… 1
   The Colors of His Love *Dr. Karina J. Belkin* 2
   Reality's Kiss *Dr. Karina J. Belkin* 4
   Your Immortal Reality *Dr. Karina J. Belkin* 6
   The Repented Affair *Dr. Karina J. Belkin* 8
   The Weeping Willow *Dr. Karina J. Belkin* 9
   Crowned An Aphrodisiac *Dr. Karina J. Belkin* 10
   Marriage of the Priest *Dr. Karina J. Belkin* 11
   Nature's Sublime Gift *Dr. Karina J. Belkin* 12
   Rain's Magical Dance *Dr. Karina J. Belkin* 13
   Let Me Be… *Dr. Karina J. Belkin* 14
   One with My Dance *Dr. Karina J. Belkin* 15
   Casa La Femme *Dr. Karina J. Belkin* 16
   Hot Air Balloon *Elric Bowdean* 18
   No More Pain *Elric Bowdean* 19
   Darkness Within *Elric Bowdean* 20
   Almond Blossoms *Elric Bowdean* 21
   Wonderful Day *Elric Bowdean* 22
   Plastic Flowers *Elric Bowdean* 23
   Needing Each Other *Elric Bowdean* 24
   Crying for my child *Elric Bowdean* 26
   Kaleidoscope *Elric Bowdean* 27
   Love's Heavy Hand *Elric Bowdean* 28
   Crossroads *Elric Bowdean* 29
   The Wine Press *Michael Cotner* 30
   Regrets *Michael Cotner* 32
   My Backyard *Michael Cotner* 34
   Morning Prayers *Michael Cotner* 35
   My Beloved *Michael Cotner* 36

Winter of the Soul *Michael Cotner*	38
The Warrior's Call *Michael Cotner*	39
Wistful Dreams *Michael Cotner*	40
Ramparts of the Heart *Michael Cotner*	41
The Fall of Baldor Jarlsbane *Michael Cotner*	42
Spring Blossoms in Stone Gardens *Timothy Michael Flaherty*	48
In This Day *Timothy Michael Flaherty*	50
Brush Strokes in D Minor *Timothy Michael Flaherty*	52
Tuesday's Butterfly *Timothy Michael Flaherty*	54
Tears Forever *James M. Furber*	56
Writer's Child *James M. Furber*	57
Time *James M. Furber*	58
Hands I Pass Along the Way *James M. Furber*	60
Lifetime Lost *James M. Furber*	62
Dance Forever *James M. Furber*	64
Dawgone Dawg *James M. Furber*	65
Our Wall *James M. Furber*	66
Forever in his Heart *James M. Furber*	67
Cry Little Child *James M. Furber*	68
The Confession *James M. Furber*	69
The Poet *James Hastings*	70
A Campfire Sonnet *James Hastings*	71
This Blessed Curse *James Hastings*	72
Very Little *James Hastings*	73
The Only Force No Man Can Tame *James Hastings*	74
Her Anniversary *James Hastings*	75
Tell Me, Old Man *James Hastings*	76
A Walk Through the Old Cemetery *James Hastings*	77
The Ballad of Charles Nobody *James Hastings*	78
The Changing of Tides on a Starry Night *James Hastings*	79
One Star *James Hastings*	80
When I am But Ashes *James Hastings*	81
The Mountain's Call *James Hastings*	82
Your Love *Hannah Hastings*	83
Would You? *Hannah Hastings*	84
The Art of the Skies *Hannah Hastings*	85
The Prayer of a Child *Hannah Hastings*	86
Mother, please don't cry for me *Robert Lock*	88

The War Horse *Robert Lock*	90
My Few Words to You *Robert Lock*	92
The Galleon *Robert Lock*	93
Gelert's Return *Robert Lock*	94
The Lonely Teddy Bear *Robert Lock*	95
Y Ddraig Goch (The Red Dragon) *Robert Lock*	96
I am Moby Dick *Robert Lock*	97
The Little Geisha *Robert Lock*	98
A Texan Iliad *Robert Lock*	100
Soldier's Tears *Robert Lock*	101
The Serpent Smile *Robert Lock*	102
Father, Thank You *Robert Lock*	103
Follicly Challenged *Robert Lock*	104
This Ring hath no Hand *Robert Lock*	105
Rural Kentucky Morning *Mark Manis*	107
Another Life *Mark Manis*	108
Scarred *Mark Manis*	109
HANDICAPPED *Mark Manis*	110
The Planting *Mark Manis*	111
A Kiss of Moonlight *Mark Manis*	112
Grief and Acceptance *Mark Manis*	114
The Dawning *Mark Manis*	115
Under Luna's Sky *Mark Manis*	116
Barren Road of Enlightenment *Mark Manis*	117
Under the Stars *Mark Manis*	118
Another Morning *Mark Manis*	119
Light Touch *Mark Manis*	120
Simple Pleasures *Mark Manis*	121
Connections of Water *Mark Manis*	122
The Production Line *James Oldfield*	124
The Muse *James Oldfield*	125
Mr. Balloon *James Oldfield*	126
The Door *James Oldfield*	127
The Scythe *James Oldfield*	128
Finity's End *James Oldfield*	130
Yesterday's Tears *James Oldfield*	134
Samael *James Oldfield*	136
The Hourglass *James Oldfield*	138

Birdsong *James Oldfield*	141
Bliss *James Oldfield*	142
The Tiger *James Oldfield*	144
The Samurai *James Oldfield*	146
The Shopping *James Oldfield*	148
Men of Greed *Alexander Pavelich*	150
I Fly *Alexander Pavelich*	152
The Bard *Alexander Pavelich*	153
Heart of the Forest *Alexander Pavelich*	154
Begin Anew *Cynthia Jeanne Rider*	155
Secret Garden *Cynthia Jeanne Rider*	156
Secrets Locked Inside *Cynthia Jeanne Rider*	158
Queen Anne's Lace *Cynthia Jeanne Rider*	159
Gecko's Tale *Cynthia Jeanne Rider*	160
Golden Embers *Cynthia Jeanne Rider*	162
Tending My Garden *Cynthia Jeanne Rider*	163
Life Long Friend *Cynthia Jeanne Rider*	165
A Lonely Road *Cynthia Jeanne Rider*	167
Golden Sweater *Cynthia Jeanne Rider*	168
Double Delight *Cynthia Jeanne Rider*	169
Evening Sky *Cynthia Jeanne Rider*	170
Virtuosity *Cynthia Jeanne Rider*	171
Spring Whimsy *Cynthia Jeanne Rider*	172
Taste The Sky *Cynthia Jeanne Rider*	173
Outpouring *Lorraine R. Sautner*	175
The Alchemist *Lorraine R. Sautner*	176
Bird of Jove *Lorraine R. Sautner*	178
Sanctum Sanctorum *Lorraine R. Sautner*	179
The Prayer *Lorraine R. Sautner*	180
A Goddess' Quandary *Jennifer Penix-Taylor*	182
Alone *Jennifer Penix-Taylor*	184
Silent Beauty *Jennifer Penix-Taylor*	186
The Seduction of Eve *Jennifer Penix-Taylor*	187
War's Mistress *Jennifer Penix-Taylor*	188
The Connoisseur *Sherri A. Tillman*	190
Archetypal Dreamtime *Sherri A. Tillman*	192
Wild and Tender Wisdoms *Sherri A. Tillman*	195
Feast of Innocents/ Blessed Be Iago *Sherri A. Tillman*	196

Dialogue with My Inner Medusa *Sherri A. Tillman* 200
My Secret Garden *Sherri A. Tillman* 202
Soul Deep ... Time *Sherri A. Tillman* 206
To Sculpt A Lover *Sherri A. Tillman* 208
Impassioned Spirits *Liza Throgmorton* 211
New Beginnings *Liza Throgmorton* 212
Fear Thunders *Liza Throgmorton* 213
Simply Sam *Liza Throgmorton* 214
Reaching out *Liza Throgmorton* 218
Love' Last Promise *Liza Throgmorton* 220
First Night Home *Nora D. Watterson* 222
The Prowler *Nora D. Watterson* 223
The Dreaming *Nora D. Watterson* 224
Etchings in the Glass *Nora D. Watterson* 226
I Speak To You *Nora D. Watterson* 227

Biographies – Introducing the Authors 229

About the Author 235

Publisher's Choice...

Dr. Karina J. Belkin	Colors of His Love
Elric Bowdean	Plastic Flowers
Michael Cotner	The Fall of Baldor Jarlsbane
Timothy Michael Flaherty	Spring Blossoms in Stone Gardens
James Furber	Tears Forever
James Hastings	The Poet
Hannah Hastings	Would You?
Robert Lock	I am Moby Dick
Mark Allan Manis	Rural Kentucky Morning
James Hedley Oldfield	Mr. Balloon
Alexander Pavelich	Men of Greed
Cynthia Jeanne Rider	Life Long Friend
Lorraine R. Sautner	The Alchemist
Jennifer Penix-Taylor	War's Mistress
Sherri A. Tillman	The Connoisseur
Lisa Throgmorton	Chance's Child
Nora D Watterson	The Prowler

Dr. Karina J. Belkin

The Colors of His Love

In that stark white room, cold as ice, listless he lay.
Eyes of suffering and humility engraved his face.
A meticulous portrait of two world wars fought and won.
Elevated ranks, medals and honors on the field and in life.
The shadows of tragic loss, his youngest daughter gone,
Like a root ripped out from under an oak tree.

Within those plain white walls spotlessly painted,
I recalled him being solid as a mountain,
Straight as a beam of light.
A lieutenant, pilot, perfectionist and workaholic,
In the body of a Russian teddy bear.

Looking at that bare white floor with faultless squares,
Memories embraced me like a charming lullaby.
Of nature walks and nightly talks.
The way he called me, "dearest daughter",
Echoed his affections through my soul.
Generous and warm,
He was grander than the sun for my darker days.

On that hard white bed meticulously made,
He lay so vulnerable, ill and torn apart.
Lung failure taking my teddy bear's life.
My heart warned me of this last goodbye.
Trembling, I told him, "I love you".

Dr. Karina J. Belkin

The Colors of His Love (continued)

Selfish tears rained from my altruistic eyes.
Analgesically convincing myself and him,
"eighty-one is still young".
I held his rough shaking hand.
He reassured me smiling deliberately.
Knowing his suffering would cease, I let him go.
His heart spoke tranquility, as it stopped beating.

In that stark white room, cold as ice,
His eyes closed to pain and suffering.
The colors of his love painted a perfect rainbow,
Giving that white room, those walls,
That floor and that bed… the colors of his life.

Dr. Karina J. Belkin

Reality's Kiss

He is ecstatic from the music
I am seduced by it
He feels its power over me
I fall submissive to it

He pierces me with his stare
I am mesmerized
He speaks in tongues of desire
I can read his mind

He approaches me
I welcome him seductively
He invites me to dance
I accept his sexy proposal

He touches my swaying hips as we move
I feel his tribal demeanor expanding
He whispers softly into my ear
I collapse in overwhelming desire

His lips play my mouth like a flute
I tune in to his sultry song
His wet kiss becomes the perfect melody
I become the perfect dancer

He asks me to leave with him
I give in to his desires
His ego is lifted
I continue to feed it, one bite at a time

Dr. Karina J. Belkin

Reality's Kiss (continued)

He takes me home
In his arms, I am at home
He leads me
I follow his every move

He takes off my clothing
But, I undress his inhibitions
He makes love to me all night long
I am handcuffed to his passions

He falls into a slumber
I meet him in my dreams
He suddenly awakens
As do I…to reality's kiss

Dr. Karina J. Belkin

Your Immortal Reality

Many illusions exist on earth,
But our love is real.
Being of celestial origin,
It is more genuine than a mountain's peak,
Protruding through the clouds;

As predictable as the sunrise
On the ocean's waist line;
Unfathomable like the deepest abyss.
As indisputable as heaven's serenity.

I have died numerous times
To live in this love for you.
I have lived many lives
To be yours immortally.

If ever you were taken from me,
My love would discover you again.
And after I die,
I would be reborn
To find you yet again.

Out of my love,
The creation of your reality
Would be born.

Dr. Karina J. Belkin

Your Immortal Reality (continued)

The depths of my heart
Are as vast as the universe.
The key to my heart is your soul.
The birth of our reality,
Is the death of your illusions.

Part with the mirage
Of the sands of time.
Our fusion is eternal.
Marry the endless cosmos of our love.
Surrender to my unequivocal feelings
And realize that I am your immortal reality.

Dr. Karina J. Belkin

The Repented Affair

Affliction of rejection rushes through my veins.
Infernal charm, smoldering manipulation ignited,
Like a burning injection of his vile venom,
Poisoning my once peaceful dwellings of stability.

Mesmerizing my love, violating a holy bond,
Selfish delectation of sin, destroying innocence.
Taunting my guilty heart, filled with fire,
Of promised passion but received torment.

Pleasure laced with pain, forming cruelty,
From tears of sexual ecstasy pouring,
On a dry lonely world in my season of drought,
Where every drop enlivened new hopes.

Hiding behind the sky in its grandeur,
Seducing my mind with pitiless deception.
Ripped dreams of tomorrow called yesterday,
Buried in infertile soil, rotting, a corpse of our love.

Memories of loss destroying my world,
Leaving me, alone and robbed of my pride.
Solid family shattered into specks of dust,
To dwell forever… on my repented affair.

Dr. Karina J. Belkin

The Weeping Willow

A weeping willow's dangling branches,
Blow from side to side in the callous wind.
Thirsty roots loosening in the crumbling dry earth,
Swaying like a mourner in the midst of his pain.

A pompous melody accompanying,
The wind's nonchalance is no longer heard
By the willow, deafened in its grief.
Blinded by the reservoir of darkness in its heart.

Shedding its leaves with movements of despair,
Naked it dwells, in the forest of its loneliness.
Crying in the company of the wanton wind,
Struggling for comfort, realizing its farewell.

Singing its own song, the unsympathetic wind
Hears not the tears of liberation blowing away,
Never reaching the observing ground to solidify
The arid soil in which the weeping willow stands…falling alone.

Dr. Karina J. Belkin

Crowned An Aphrodisiac

Lip licking, fresh pasta spirals, drizzled with amore
Basil, garlic, pine nut pesto, seducing me galore

Creamy, chewy mushrooms are embracing every curl
Rolling on my pink tongue in a most delicious swirl

Roasted pepper coulee, drizzled all around the plate
Eyes are closed in heavy passion, on this culinary date

Jasmine tea of soothing scents, undressing my appetite
Mango-sorbet paradise massaging my palette just right

Dark chocolate, spongy heaven, moist with decadence
Sprinkled showers of roasted nuts in ecstasy immense

Tangy sweet red raspberry sauce, enchanting every bite
Edible flowers adorning plates, ensuring the perfect sight

Panting, moaning, heavy breathing, with each orgasmic meal
Taking my time with every bite, for all my sense's appeal

Delicious wonderland of rapture, deserving a sensual plaque
Food prepared with love and heat, is crowned an aphrodisiac

Dr. Karina J. Belkin

Marriage of the Priest

Seven cherubs singing an aria
By the celestial light.
It is in his voice, a lullaby,
Serene as a butterfly's flight.

Blessed with a heart that keeps
His spirit on the narrow path.
Far from a soul's destruction,
Destined within God's wrath.

Sacrificing self in struggle,
Pleasures saved for paradise,
Lonely life of altruism,
Temptation will not entice.

Sapphire waterfalls of wisdom,
Diamond oceans of love,
With him flies the shadow
Of The Great White Dove.

When His wings embrace his being,
Opening his sightless eyes,
He will be as one with Eden,
His wife, the heavenly skies.

Dr. Karina J. Belkin

Nature's Sublime Gift

Aroused by sunrise's amber kiss,
An imprint of awakening brilliance,
Infinite rays of divinity and warmth
Stimulating the rapture of living in the day.

Delighted by a sprinkling shower,
Open mouthed, I capture the sweet mist,
Dancing off my body's infernal heat,
To the melody of nature's tango.

Embraced by the wind's cool breeze
Benevolently blowing fresh scents
Of blooming lilac and dew droplets,
Collage sitting in the vase of my heart.

Made love to by smooth ocean waves,
Rhythmically thrusting salty spectacles,
Teasing the pearly white sea shores
As my footprints erase into perfection.

Pampered by sunset's rusty panorama,
Enchanting canvas of untamed beauty,
Casting its sultry ambiance of mystique,
It feeds nature's sublime gifts into the night.

Dr. Karina J. Belkin

Rain's Magical Dance

Rain's tantalizing song, tapping, thumping,
Throwing itself abound in tribal dance
Clear magical droplets of exhilaration
Purifying my soul in its cleansing ritual

Cool shower, heat-quenching magic
Lifting my body with its hypnotic rhythm
Refreshing the essence of my bliss
Replenishing thirst for its symphony

Cascading from euphoric clouds
Singing, humming, purring as they collapse
Like a mirror, reflecting my mind's serenity
The finale of each droplet uniting in silence

Dr. Karina J. Belkin

Let Me Be…

Let me be your queen…
Adorned with magnificent jewels of triumph,
Placing a majestic crown over your head,
Protecting you with my enormous strength,
From all predatory harm, in your kingdom,
Where your castle is my heart.

Let me be your angel…
Wide winged, gentle and exuding light.
Leading you on the path towards illumination,
Taking you away from darkness and pain,
Into the candescent chambers of my soul.

Let me be your twin flame…
Acknowledging our immaculate creation.
Before heaven and the cosmos as sublime,
From a single spark of God's love,
A flame resistant to all of earth's elements.

Let me be your confidant…
Eternally loyal and forever silent.
Hearing, listening, and understanding at a glimpse,
Giving you, company, compassion and support,
Accepting nothing in return but your happiness.

Dr. Karina J. Belkin

One with My Dance

Dancing in the heat of your desert's song,
I am your secret tantalizer, an enigma of sensual bliss,
Your vision of exotic beauty made manifest.
Transparent veils of allure cover my face.
Fine silk barely embraces my gold-dusted body.

My waist reveals the shape of a guitar,
Strumming the chords of your delight.
As I dance to entice your love,
Bells around my ankles ring,
Celebrating my body's thousand and one sensual movements.

My tantalizing eyes, brown, almond-shaped, are painted,
In colors of the darkest and deepest seduction.
A red ruby of tantra kisses my third eye.
Jewels of all gods adorn my skin,
As does perfume of a distant field of jasmine.

Dancing to the voice of your passions,
The curves of my body reveal themselves,
Moving like the ocean's cool waves,
Sizzling against your body's heat;
My secret chambers open to embrace your song.

Dancing on the sands of your desire,
You are now naked in me.
As the sun sets over your desert,
I am one with your pleasure,
And you are one… with my dance.

Dr. Karina J. Belkin

Casa La Femme

Spices of Morocco fill the air like wine's
Inebriating scents, rich in seduction.
Bodies intertwined under a canopy
Of flowing transparent satin shimmering,
Like tiny stars flying across the night sky,
Hovering over sultry earth tones,
Tent of a hundred pillows of temptation.

Arabesque beats hit erogenous zones,
Like the Red Sea's waves pounding
Against unstable rocks of an aroused sea shore,
Swallowing them into the wet abyss of sensuality,
Where they are pulled into the depths
Of passion's heart and chiseled into oneness.
Alluring dance of enchantment.

Flickering candles infused with cinnamon bark.
Flames swaying like a belly dancer's hips.
Changing the night into iridescent desire,
Igniting appetites of bodily hunger,
Revealing shadows of departing inhibitions,
As they're consumed into the endless flames.
Pillars of heat melting innocence.

Tarbuka drums vibrating, like electricity
Through two bodies engulfing their boundaries,
Like snakes swirling around one another,
Lost in the ambience of overwhelming urges.
On one Arabian night under a majestic tent,
Tasting temptation and swimming in enchantment,
While burning away their unnecessary innocence.

C.J. Rider

Elric Bowdean

Hot Air Balloon

Floating above, ball of life,
Free from mortal bonds,
Heat filled orbs dotting the sky
Filling me with illusions of joy,
Colors of the rainbow
Dancing amongst the clouds.
Blown about upon the wind of chance?

Freedom seen by dwellers below,
Causing them to desire its course.
Grounded by its earthly ties,
Still has no regrets of the day.
Always needing more to keep adrift,
yet finding its strength in the elements.
The hunger for fire is never satisfied.

Many shapes to please our view,
Favorite is the dew drop shape,
Reminding me of colored rain ascending from earth.
Hot air balloons drifting aimlessly,
Living life to the fullest amongst men.
With only one thought, one concern, where to land.

Elric Bowdean

No More Pain

Sweet nothings whispered upon neglectful ears
Brings untold satisfaction to a dysfunctional soul.
I breathe my last words of love on her neck,
Shrinking back knowing no reply will be given
Screaming inside from the lack of affection.

Love filled house belied by actions shown.
Why do I keep reaching out to you?
How long will your lies make me feel small?
What will be the straw that sets you off?
Questions I know the answers, still I ponder over.

Air of discontent permeates my every breath.
I inhale deeply, starved by lack of oxygen
Igniting a passion of loathing for all.
Feelings locked up so tight I have become hard.
Children flee from attitude of stone.

Hatred ripe for sewing love's deceiving hand,
Dealt from the bottom of your cheating soul.
Hostility leaves its unseen scars of amputation
Upon my psyche, left without concern for my mind,
Disdained by the act of picking up mental pieces.

Love lost to make room for your pride.
Pushed aside, a crumb held out, token of what could be.
Our lackluster marriage held together by kids,
Screaming into the night hoping, praying,
For no more feelings, no more cares, no more pain.

Elric Bowdean

Darkness Within

Dreams occupy my mind
of the day that we will be united
in a joy unbounded upon earth.
I awake to find that you are gone.

I fantasize that my wishes would come true,
For then you would be mine,
our sorrows forever tossed away.
Hallucinations dispel my desires.

Fulfillment of my passions
would bring contentment to my life
and happiness from these thoughts.
Yet the void within is never filled.

Pain seeps into my soul,
feelings tangled within
leaving only a drug-induced withdrawal
To remind me of wanting more.

Knowing that I am dead within,
Still I put myself upon the altar,
wondering if my sacrifice
will bring true hope or oblivion.

Celestial bodies in the heavens
bring forth sparkles in my eye.
Time reveals that it is only
light from dying stars.

Without your illumination,
darkness is all that is left
surrounding my heart,
leaving a black hole where light shone.

Elric Bowdean

Almond Blossoms

Early spring we would walk hand in hand among the almond trees.
Sweet fragrances from flowers in full bloom delighted our senses.
Peacefulness filled our lives in that unforgettable moment.

In awe we watched the serene landscape awaken before us.
The morning breeze embraced the blossoms and made them dance.
Petals floated about us, slowly drifting earth bound for our enjoyment.

Pinkish white flowers piled up around us twirling about our feet.
My true love by my side, the earth seemed to stand still for us.
We watched in amazement at the scene of beauty we had found.

Yet compared to her, this wondrous scene paled to her beauty.
Her fire-blue eyes were highlighted by petals of white in her hair.
The ambiance she brought to this place will forever be with me.

I have often tried to reclaim that magical moment in my life.
Time that we spent in each other's arms, watching the world
passing us by as we walked among the almond blossoms

Elric Bowdean

Wonderful Day

Salt in the air from waves crashing upon the shore.
Awaken inner desires of peace so long forgotten.
Sand being sucked out from underneath me.
Reminds me I am alive and not full of heartless actions.
Joy of life begins to radiate from me as the sun rises.

Songs of hunger cry out from the neighborhood gulls
As my wife feeds them persimmon cookies.
We laugh; at least we have found someone who enjoys them.
I look on in amazement at the fighting that peruses
And am reminded how petty my hateful words have been.

Fishermen stuffing their traps full of fish carcasses.
Hoping for the big haul as they lower their nets.
We are all in excitement of eating fresh crab tonight.

The sites we see at San Francisco Bay,
Golden Gate Bridge painted Reddish orange.
Alcatraz Prison a monument and eyesore all in one.

Seals and jellyfish are not the strangest sites to see.
We marvel, we gawk, "Did you see that mans hair?
How many studs do you think she had?"
My inner self finds contentment in the face of the oddities
We have perceived, from them; I too can still see my own growth.

Tired and worn out time to head on home,
Memories stored away to tell for another day.
Crabs a crackin', fresh butter, man these are good.
A wonderful day overall, not that it was above average,
I was able to get out of myself and say I am glad to be

Elric Bowdean

Plastic Flowers

My brother's death brought great sadness,
Tears stream down upon disconnected faces.
Sorrow blooms where happiness once grew.
Wondering what would have been, could have been.

Memorial placed upon the roadside.
Flowers and candles adorn the sidewalk.
Every day more plastic flowers are placed.
By hearts stricken in grief, mourning the loss.

A satin-lined box of wood, his final resting place,
Holds the remains of unfulfilled love.
All shuffle by for one final look.
A morbid touch from those left behind.

His final trip with friends in tow,
As the hearse makes its way to the grave.
Pain grows as they slowly lower him down.
Soft goodbyes while tears flow, roses fall.

You touched so many in your life.
Just think at the tender age of seventeen.
They try to tell me plastic flowers do not grow.
Yet everyday I find more and more.

Elric Bowdean

Needing Each Other

Cradling a teddy bear in your arms wanting me,
I crawl into bed late, as you sleep peacefully.
Waiting for your mate, limbs wrap around my body.
Reminding me of what a lucky man I am.

In the middle of the night I awaken
From pleasant dreams and desires of you.
Terror rips through me; heart implodes
Finding empty space next to me.

I rush out to find you sitting in the dark.
Tears running down your cheeks.
Holding you, what's wrong? How can I help?
You open up, I listen, I speak softly, I cry along.

Be-darken the sun becomes next to your light,
Moments are enlightened by your glow.
Showing me the way I ought to walk
Helping me not to stumble on my way.

Ripped from your side to make a living,
The day drags on away from you.
At home you are anticipating your man
Frantic if I arrive a little late.

Long hug; longer kiss, holding you in my arms
Never wanting to let you go.
As we merge back into one soul.
All of the day's concerns melt away.

Elric Bowdean

Needing Each Other (continued)

Rose petals shower down on my skin
As your lips slowly press against me,
Running chills of deep seeded passion.
Your kisses awaken my urgency for more.

Purest gold is your whisper next to my ear.
We cuddle ever so close; sleep overtakes me,
Embraced in your arms my souls resting place.
Dreams are meant for others, yet I am fulfilled.

Elric Bowdean

Crying for my child

A gentle touch, causing each other to become intoxicated.
Lost in time's immense grasp upon our reality.
Love and passion cloud our young, eager minds.
Kisses, moments full of joy and a child is conceived.

A new reality emerges as we realize our treasure.
Within my love our future, our hopes of tomorrow,
The wonders he or she will bring still unknown.
Before us, life's curiosities are beginning to unfold.

Euphoria cut short, life's thread ruptured, soul torn away.
Joy's jewel shattered into shards, breaking clay hearts.
We cry out in anguish borne of the loss of one.
Asking, "Why? Oh why? Please take me instead!"

Childless curdles our spirits and torches our hearts.
Knowledge of what could have, should have been,
Cuts deeper than words, leaving scars unseen.
Asking, "Why is life so cruel to take away our son?"

Tears begin to run down my cheeks, landing on this poem,
As I wonder how my boy's life would have changed me.
I weep not only for my loss, but also for yours,
And still I cry out "Take me! Please, take me!"

Kaleidoscope

Shattered eyes giving kaleidoscope view,
Color blind so no pleasure is received.
Images fractured leaving misery painted in gray.
Where did the hue of passion go?
All love drained through cracked orbs.

Appendages become broken reaching out to you,
Fists cry in anguish at the hardness they met.
For within you a soul I could not find.
They return empty, blooded stumps;
Warmth was drained from the coldness found.

The littlest member causing me great pain,
Cut it off, never to speak again, a gift.
Lies I weave to keep the flow of love alive.
Hollow, void, translucent screams come forth;
Only empty echoes of past deceptions are left.

Intestines careen forward demanding a release,
Aching to be gutted from their prison.
Awakening to violence, erupting, tearing me asunder.
Just for the pleasure of having you next to me.
When will the consumption end?

A whirlwind I live leaves me wondering,
When will the day come that my blood flows no more?
For the color of crimson is not seen by me.
Yet smeared upon your name, my life force ends.
No longer spinning, the kaleidoscope only sees red.

Elric Bowdean

Love's Heavy Hand

Love's heavy hand, lying upon me like a millstone,
Crushing, grinding me into powder under its weight.
Cleansed of all impurities, refined to her satisfaction.
Molded as if dough, into her designs and desires.

Roses I give, hoping to rekindle an exhausted flame,
Set in a golden vase to emphasize our cherished bond.
The vase was sold, flowers left upon the table to die,
Petals littering the surface, reminding me of failed love.

Incantations made in the dark to hide my once-caring heart.
Chanting about imaginary deeds, giving illusion of hope.
Reciting vows trying to recall why we stay together.
Your lack of interest leaves me bitter and hollow.

She pulls me into her chest and orders me to listen;
Asking me, do you hear it? "I told you, it only beats for you."
Forced to stay against her torso, I begin to suffocate.
Fighting for independent thought, all I hear is beating.

Solitude sets in from lack of friendship,
Denied freedoms of thought and of choice.
Demands placed so high no true hope can be seen.
Love's heavy hand, is killing me.

Elric Bowdean

Crossroads

Standing at crossroads, love's dividing marker.
Choices made demands placed between two.
Fighting to keep each other in our separate lives.

Cruelty is our fate, always parting.
Neither willing to change, desiring the other to follow,
A metamorphosis we wish upon one another.

Optimistic is our outlook on the future.
While mayflies change just to mate and die,
Death, the state of separateness, we live day by day.

Fears we air about living separately.
Anxiety blossoms, depression sets in,
Love's thieving hand, wrenches our lives apart!

Despair springs forth, multiplying like weeds.
Thistles choking all growth we strive to make.
Saying goodbye is our only recourse.

Eyes dancing as desire grows for love.
Hearts yearning, demanding togetherness,
Yet our tongues speak words we hate to hear.

We walk away from each other on different roads.
No hugs, no kisses, just regrets.
Wondering…will our paths ever cross again?

Michael Cotner

The Wine Press

Your love is like divers wine.
Oft times a dark and heavy Merlot
drawn from the bleeding cuts inflicted
by razor sharp words spoke in anger.

Its flavor and bouquet unpalatable
as sour vinegar squeezed from a sop.
Pressed from the grapes of seething bitterness.
Bottled up in casks of unforgiveness.

Other times a light and joyful Sauvignon Blanc.
Bursting forth from the well spring of our wants.
Wrapped in carnal desires and lust,
intoxicating and refreshing to the soul.

Its aroma and savor a delicacy.
Sweet as honey from the comb.
Pressed from the grapes of scintillating passions,
poured out in copious goblets of adoration.

In times past, a clear sparkling Asti.
Cascading in fountains of virgin purity.
Displayed as decoration and adornment,
a priceless pearl among innumerable grains of sand.

Its effervescence a sensual delight.
Crisp and clean as mountain snows.
Pressed from the grapes of oath bound vows,
served in crevasses of honor and fidelity.

Michael Cotner

The Wine Press (continued)

Yet, always and forever, a prized Dom Perrier.
Aged in the cellar of our conjoined life.
A treasure only enjoyed by the sharing,
testimonial to the enduring journey.

Its piquancy alive with robust pleasure.
Vibrant and alluring as ocean swells.
Pressed from the grapes of enduring friendship,
sipped from the chalice of selfless devotion.

Michael Cotner

Regrets

In my heart I have built
a castle strong and true.
Its foundations laid on pain and guilt,
and fond memories of you.

There are no banners flying
upon the spires tall
and only voices crying
echo through the musty hall.

Within the hearth no fires burn
to warm the empty rooms
where ghostly shadows, boiling, churn
and cobwebs hang in gloom.

No life stirs inside
this castle cold and stark
save the soul that hides
quietly cowering in the dark.

Remembering all the times
when lovers danced and played,
reciting all the rhymes
that lovers often trade.

No stolen kiss or shared embrace,
beneath the waxen moon,
is left for me to mark the place
our love was lost so soon.

Michael Cotner

Regrets (continued)

Never will this castle bloom
with loves abounding grace
enclosed I am with pending doom
shut in without a trace.

If only I had given you
the moments we shared best
perhaps I'd have won love true
and been forever blessed.

Michael Cotner

My Backyard

Meadows verdant, green and rolling
covered in Daisy, Daffodil, and Kings Foil
stretch for miles along the horizon.

Orchards of ripe plum and pear
stand in rows like sentries,
guardians to some lost, forbidden city.

Fields laden with fruit of the vine and stalk
cover the caricature of the earth
in richness and bounty untold.

Canyons, sheer and hard, solid granite,
thrust to the heavens above, where the sky,
blue as the deepest lake at sunset, reigns as lord over all.

Sequoia, the giant redwood, oldest of trees,
rooted upon the foundations of the world;
support the clouds with their canopies.

As I sit and survey all that I can,
the glorious panorama too spectacular to take in,
I hear a distant voice calling me…

"Honey, dinner's ready!"

The sequoia shrink to hoary oak and maple.
The canyons pale to concrete grain elevators.
The fields of ripe fruit fade to seed corn and soybeans.
The orchard becomes a lonely apple tree
and the meadow flowers are but lowly dandelions.

Such is the beauty of a daydream in my backyard.

Michael Cotner

Morning Prayers

With the coming of the dawn,
so breaks another day.
A vibrant new beginning
to life and love and play.

Though my eyes still heavy
from my slumbered rest,
as they gently open,
I see how God has blessed.

The sun shines through my window
to warm my heart and face.
I couldn't be more happy
in any other place.

I hear my children playing,
laughing as they run.
What joy there is in toys and games
and summer morning fun.

My wife's still gently sleeping,
dreaming on my shoulder.
Comforted by the way,
I so dearly kiss and hold her.

As the days move steadily on,
I'll wake each time with Christ the King,
one more day to see His glory,
one more day His praise to sing.

Michael Cotner

My Beloved

Apollo, robed in radiant splendor, chariot blazing,
bowed low in humble supplication.
Clouds burst into flame at his passing,
blue sky tinged in ochre and amethyst became his canvas,
and my thoughts turned to you, my beloved.

Dionysis, irreverent Dionysis,
even though you did stamp and press
the most enchanted of wines,
even if 'twas made of thine own life's blood,
nair would it taste as sweet as my beloved's lips.

And you, vain and beautiful Aphrodite,
fairest of all Olympus, jealousy does not become you.
Never hast thy beauty known an equal,
but 'tis better thou cast thine eyes aside
lest thou gaze upon my beloved.

What sayest thou mighty Zeus?
What love hast thou shared that could measure?
One whose head is turned so easily
knows more of folly than of love.

And you, Athena, what dost thou know of love?
I will not pray to you to invoke some spell or magic.
I have no need of your bewitchments,
vapors that swirl in the wind and vanish,
dissolving to oblivion.

Michael Cotner

My Beloved (continued)

For one reason only I boast so mightily
against the Pantheon of Greece:
When Mount Olympus is drifting sand, and all of its gods
become dim shadows in the minds of men,
and my bones are but dust,

Even unto the passing of the earth and moon and stars,
there, woven into the fabric of the universe,
will be forever bound the words
I love you, my beloved.

Michael Cotner

Winter of the Soul

Lifeless lies my soul
in dark and slumbering rest,
waiting for eternity to pass
beyond life's yearning quest.

Living life behind a mask
that hides my loss and pain.
Devoid of any joyful hope
of finding love's refrain.

Icy winds howl like ravenous wolves
freezing tears before they fall.
Hellish icicles show the grief
of lost love's dreadful pall.

Darkness blankets my heart and soul
with binding fetters tight,
and without the hope of coming dawn
despair thrives in endless night.

No pain of mortal man's device
could compare to what I feel,
possessing not your passionate love
my heart melts like molten steel.

Elusive is the lightest touch
of passion's sweet embrace.
Always looking far and wide
to find your charm and grace.

Poured out upon the barren ground,
my soul waits with boundless blame.
To restore me from Hell's dark bonds
you need only call my name.

Michael Cotner

The Warrior's Call

Upon the dry, broken ground
a mother's tears do fall.
Her son upon the battlefield
answered the warrior's call.

His life, his path before him
as a child was laid,
and with his life and limb
the price of freedom paid.

And in a battle begun
before the earth was born,
he fought a fight he could not win
with sword and shield alone.

But with enduring faith and love
he walked to meet his foe.
A battle to the death
to pay the debt we owe.

Upon the dry, broken ground
a mother's tears do fall.
Her son upon a wooden cross
answered the warrior's call.

His life, his path before him
a living, loving sacrifice
so that those who believe in him
may have eternal life.

Michael Cotner

Wistful Dreams

In faerie tales and stories old
are princess' fair with hair of gold.
Their beauty honored in eternal song
while mortal men do lust and long,

Just for a touch or impassioned glance,
a passing embrace, a moonlight dance.
Thereby, a ray of hope doth bring
to life, to love a wistful dream,

Of soul mates lost in passions throes
entwined like vines on budding rose,
risking chance of prickling thorn
to kiss the flower morning born.

There lying in warm embrace
eternity passes without a trace,
content my head upon thy breast
forever cradled in loving rest.

And thusly so my life would end
with thoughts of love and lust to send-
me on to heavens gilded gate
and there to dream of thee and wait.

Michael Cotner

Ramparts of the Heart

She walks upon the gilded spire
of a castle cold and harshly dire.
Yet, with angelic voice she sings,
not of love and life and golden things,

but of spells and hidden magic's lost,
her soul the price to pay the cost,
for the power she doth wield
to break men's wills that they must yield.

Her siren song and beauty draws
unwary dolts into her claws
and there enslaved each man doth die
a pitiful death of a thousand lies.

So, gladly, death comes unaware
and makes its home inside her lair,
and resting there upon whetted womb
seals men's fates in lusty tomb.

– – –

She walks upon the windswept stair,
with emerald eyes and auburn hair.
She calls to me with angelic voice,
my heart entrapped without a choice.

So before I die I make this boast
and raise my glass in joyful toast.
I bow to thee upon thy throne
and bid thee make thy love well known.

For what the price of life itself,
but to savor a taste of thy womanly wealth
and there in die with peace and content
having known the time was time well spent.

Michael Cotner

The Fall of Baldor Jarlsbane

Down passage dark and cavern deep
past rancid goblin's lair.
Through tunnels dank and musty keep
to Hell's rough-hewn stair.

With golden axe and iron helm
and breast plate made of silver,
he trudged into her ghostly realm
and crossed ol' Charon's river.

Down deeper still through sticky webs,
past glowing eyes like slits,
where mortal courage wanes and ebbs,
he came upon the demon pits.

No nightmare stark could foretell
all that he would see.
The demon spawn from darkest hell
looked on him with glee.

With jagged spear and fiery dart,
they preyed upon his soul
and fury hot as Satan's heart
burned like molten coal.

The battle raged till time was lost
and still he held his ground.
A thousand demon corpse the cost,
their screams the only sound.

His axe did glow in golden light,
as radiant as the day
and there in deepest, darkest night
all fear was rolled away.

The Fall of Baldor Jarlsbane (continued)

The golden blade danced and sang
with each and every blow,
and joyous laughter pealed and rang
as bodies fell like snow.

Valiant as he fought that day,
he knew he could stand no more.
Yet, still there was a debt to pay
and vengeance he had swore.

For somewhere in this dark domain
she waited for his wrath.
Queen of sorrow, death and pain-
she'd regret she crossed his path.

Once long past in time forgot
she loved him as her King,
but evil borne within her heart
shattered their golden ring.

And evil grew within her soul,
controlling her every thought,
till hatred consumed her body whole
and destruction was all she wrought.

Now she ruled in total sin
as queen to demon hordes
and preyed upon the souls of men
as gifts from demon lords.

At last, the battle done,
no demon stood to block his way.
He knelt in thanks, the victory won,
just one last life to slay.

Michael Cotner

The Fall of Baldor Jarlsbane (continued)

He raised his head and looking past
the bodies on the floor,
saw the hellish light, at last,
shining down murky corridor.

He knew at once her lair was found
and vengeance was his own.
Axe in hand and without a sound,
he came upon her throne.

Onyx, cold and black as night,
adorned her stately crown
and beams of captured faerie light
shone on silky spiders gown.

Not a single word was spoke,
as his piercing eyes upon her fell.
What spell or magic to invoke
would serve to protect her well?

He raised his axe above his head
for one mighty crushing blow.
Soon the evil would be dead
and all the world would know.

His eyes intent upon her face,
his axe began to fall.
Her severed head would serve to grace
his barren castle wall.

But, there upon her cheek,
what glistened in the light?
A single tear of sorrow leaked
and came into his sight.

Michael Cotner

The Fall of Baldor Jarlsbane (continued)

Could it be she felt some shame
at all that she had done,
and could he now, without some blame,
do what needed done?

Down in his heart he loved her still,
that was his greatest fear,
and the greatest spell to break his will
was a single fallen tear.

C.J. Rider

Eye Candy

Timothy Michael Flaherty

Spring Blossoms in Stone Gardens

With a seed, she chose to sow
came all her dreams undertow.
A nine month term would enshroud
all the time God would allow.

In that moment of the morn
chasten to the falling gloom
for the seed, she chose to grow
sleeps in whispers in her womb.

In the kitchen singing softly
for this child she so adorned,
came the voice of shallow talking,
like a tiger slowly stalking.
In my words, she felt the sting
for her voice ceased to sing.

He called the child in that hour.
I curse the spirits gathered round her
lurking in this milky gloom.
As your tears do truly shower
for the sorrows of your womb.

In the light of early mourn
beyond the gates of all stone gardens,
is a child that's softly crying
to a mother who feels she's dying.

How to fight this milky sorrow
that lies in stillness of the morrow,
captured in the morning gloom.
I can not fill her empty womb
with the spirits in this room.

Spring Blossoms in Stone Gardens (continued)

In the kitchen of early morn
I hear you singing in my heart
to the souls of children walking,
in little footsteps slowly stalking.

Far beyond this milky gloom
hand in hand they gather round you,
to sing in whispers,
to sing in whispers to your womb.
Take from God the time he's given,
Life must live and keep on living.

These red roses are all I offer,
to his memory I am enslaved.
In the early morn of first light
I lay them gently on his grave.

Timothy Michael Flaherty

In This Day

I am here waiting for you
as you have for me many times before.

Unwilling to see you
I have passed a thousand churches
heard not a single bell.

I could have read the story
but refused to open my eyes.
Here I am trying to chase away
the last moments of this day.

In my failure to let you know I Love You,
as if I could stop minutes from passing,
hanging them on a nail.

Lost and alone
roses clutched so hard
through tissue paper pricked by thorns
changing the color in my hands.

You have flown away
in that sunset
where you cannot hear me.

Listen for me pleading
if tomorrow you should return to me,
I will be here waiting

Somewhere in this day
lost in Roosevelt Park.

Eye Candy

Timothy Michael Flaherty

Brush Strokes in D Minor

The water shuddered
as I threw a rock in the pond;
the wake pushing out
stirring the life beneath the surface.

Walking amidst the sorrows of the Holy Land…

These camouflage fatigues are heavy
like the heat bearing down on this desert.

Holding my breath I pulled my rifle up slowly
glaring through the infrared;
impressions stalking the twilight
in the summer of resolve.

Sending a rock into the pond
I watched him fall
slowly to the bottom;
pushing out the sand that lay in his path.

Continuing my escape into the life behind me,
underneath soft brush strokes of percussion…

In the kitchen, she's cooking dinner.
The girls are chasing a dog's wagging tail
running and screaming in delight;
at the near chance of catching it.

The sounds of jazz adhering to every crack
and crevice of that old house.

Timothy Michael Flaherty

Brush Strokes in D Minor (continued)

Father I call on you …
Send me home
far away from this.

Where the peace of this world
is stirring;
the peace
that throws so many rocks.

Timothy Michael Flaherty

Tuesday's Butterfly

A harmless Tuesday in this small town,
you had to be away from here
panoramic visions of a business venture
somewhere lost in the early rush of the Ohio city.

Sipping coffee on the couch,
my baby girl sleeps
in the playpen next to me.

Dried white on the outside of a paint can,
in the corner of the dining room;
a backdrop of green and teal,
left me unfinished,
alone for another day.

Imagination on three floors
innocence lost in daydreams
floats like a butterfly.
Fluttering, moving up and down
touching each life all at once.

off to the skies…

clutching a plastic airplane
my three year old flying ace
snatches handfuls of cereal
and runs up the stairs.

She is taking advantage of mom's absence.
Adorned in a long flowing silk dress
high heels, red lipstick
and a black flowered hat,
she sings to the little girl in the mirror
in the room upstairs.

Timothy Michael Flaherty

Tuesday's Butterfly (continued)

Followed by a trip to the park
peanut butter and jelly will see me
to dinner time.

Mary Wells will tune the night
softly in the front room,
when all the kids are finally
in bed asleep.

Imagination flutters in...

I am looking for a dance
in the emptiness next to me.
Mary is singing for us.

I feel you in every verse of this sweet song,
the crisp serene crackle of your voice
raises hairs on the back of my neck.
We become silhouettes on the wall
reflected in a mirror.

You are so close to me
all the things I cannot taste
I taste them just the same,
somehow, Cincinnati

James M. Furber

Tears Forever

I've finished my tears for the day.
Thinking back to those painful years,
Friends I lost so young, needlessly.
But why did I survive the fight?
I deserved no better than they.
No more grace or good fortune.

Why did I live beyond my tour?
Making it through each close encounter,
Surviving surge after surge, and attacks
So violent, I watched my friends die.
Passing before my eyes, tearful eyes;
Wondering why that bullet denied me
My right to die along with my friends.

Each day for all these many years
Remembering that I came home standing
While they returned with flags draped.
Families mourning not understanding
Why their loved ones died, so young.
I, retreating to my hiding place, ashamed
That I returned to my family alive.
Unable to explain why I couldn't share
The joy they felt that I was spared.

When will this cease to be my cross?
So many years to carry such torture;
I fear that it will never pass until my turn,
When I too die, joining them in afterlife.
Yearning to hug and cry with my brothers.
I pray they proudly stand and say to me
That they didn't die in vain, and I lived,
To shed my tears forever, so the world
Will never forget, their enormous sacrifice.

James M. Furber

Writer's Child

Take pride in words you've written.
Hold and love them like a child.
Bathe and dress these words you cherish.
Always nurture how they're styled.

Words reflect your deepest thoughts.
Anoint them well, as you intend.
Kiss them lightly in your fashion.
Give your life to what you've penned.

Let your finished works flow out;
Begin to sow where you have ploughed.
And knowing that you've scripted well;
they'll go forth and make you proud.

The world will take what you have grown;
crafted forms that you've employed.
They'll create a lifetime tribute;
forever more to be enjoyed.

James M. Furber

Time

Time in youth, it mattered not,
for I had a playful mind.
I didn't count the minutes,
they were used and left behind.

An hour lost or day that's gone,
no seconds would remain.
My days were bought with pennies
and the years I took in vain.

Time clearly has no master.
You can never stop its way.
It moves about perpetually;
an around the clock ballet.

Now time no longer favors me.
It waits not for my reply.
Just signals as it passes,
as if to say goodbye.

I fear not that time keeps moving
or that I'll be gone tomorrow.
But rather, I'm forgotten,
and time will feel no sorrow.

Eye Candy

James M. Furber

Hands I Pass Along the Way

New day, new ways to survive;
Hands out for a piece of the world.
Standing on sides of busy passes
As the people flow on by, too blind
To notice the sack and few belongings.
Rough, weathered souls, gathered
In places we simply speed on through.

Misfortune's children, living hard.
Existing where society decides,
Sleeping wherever grace permits.
Sometimes cold, sometimes wet,
Comforted only by bottled dreams.
I've often seen the tragic eyes, faces,
Knowing death to be their only hope.

Signs of pain, painted cardboard pleas-
A handout for a meal, sometimes spirits,
But nonetheless a hand extended.
Begging for a dollar dropped or two.
The disgusting looks from so many,
As they turn away, indifferent,
Angry, beggars dared approach at all.

It's simple to legislate, nod your heads;
Turn your troubles to someone else.
Ignore the scent and ugly views,
But it will never end the constant flow.
Turning blind eyes, averting pain,
Never cures the homeless patient,
Doesn't make the 'problem' go away.

James M. Furber

Hands I Pass Along the Way (continued)

Next time you venture out and perhaps
Encounter the homeless beggar, hand out.
Don't turn your eyes away, distraught;
Rather look and imagine you are there.
But for the grace of God, just maybe,
Someday the hand I pass along the way,
Through some misfortune, may be yours.

James M. Furber

Lifetime Lost

He was an authoritative man;
Strong and controlling,
And he frightened me.
Unless I was spoken to,
I dared not converse.
Constantly afraid
Of saying the wrong thing;
Looking like a fool,
And fearing I would fail.

I never questioned my father.
It mattered only that I live his way.
Childhood to manhood,
Nothing ever changed.
Out of respect, I followed him.
Strange this insecurity,
He cultivated in me.
Never did he say he loved me
Or he was proud of my successes.

He grew older, softer,
But kept the façade,
Well into my adulthood.
Still trying to master his domain,
Unyielding, the crusty old man,
Continued to affect my balance.
Father would always be the same,
Refusing to express his feelings.
No matter, I loved him quietly.

James M. Furber

Lifetime Lost (continued)

He died well before his time,
Too far away to be by his side,
I regretted not getting to him in time.
My fault, I didn't get there sooner.
I sat in his house and cried,
Years of emotions pouring out.
Why so much emotion in death
When in life it never came?
The answer found in a letter in his box.

He feared he was an inferior man.
Never good enough as a father,
Always afraid he'd fail.
He withdrew to keep me sheltered
Because he didn't know how
To teach me to be a man.
The pain of those words, forever felt.
Two souls living by the same fears;
A lifetime lost because they couldn't share.

James M. Furber

Dance Forever

Please dance with me tonight.
Tell me how much you care.
Whisper in my ear, once again,
The words of love I cherish so.
Take my hand, and move with me,
Fused together, synchronized as one.

Hands in concert, never apart,
We glide around the dance floor,
Sprinkling our magic dust around;
If only others could share our spell;
Knowing just how much we matter,
Never stopping, not willing to let go.

Music keeps us dancing, joined eternally,
Smiling, enjoying love together.
Our hearts keeping time, beating on;
It is a wonderful dance we share.
Attraction strong and enduring,
Your eyes meet mine, it's understood.

Our dance shall last forevermore.

James M. Furber

Dawgone Dawg

I'm sitting here, watching my spouse,
Play with another, her heart stolen away.
Affections alienated, I have no chance.
Dejected, I find my love unrequited.

He entitles himself to all that I possess,
Rubbing his scent on everything he touches.
She sits transfixed, and misses not,
His mischievous runs around the house.

The arrogance of his daring jaunts,
And his cavalier brushes past my face,
On his way to another romp with mom.
He treads on ice so thin but doesn't care.

I'd throttle him, if I thought no risk,
Though I'd surely find myself run out.
At least the scoundrel would be gone,
And I'd be rid of my fiercest foe.

It's childish I know, and truly absurd
To be jealous of a furry male.
But it's not my fault, I must lament,
This dog of hers does drive me so.

Wife, I trust your love for him
Is born from a kind, and loving heart.
I know how cute some pets can be,
And he plays his part so well.

He smiles at me, and thumbs his paw,
Knowing mom has saved the day.
For after all is said and done, he knows,
Just who's boss and who's the dog.

James M. Furber

Our Wall

We watched soldiers die in place.
The taste of war we swallowed,
Cruel, beyond our youthful age.
Huddled in bunkers, praying for life,
Day upon day, hardened to war.
Thousands clashing in battles;
Brave, childlike men marching to fight.
Our youngest sons on stretchers borne,
The dead we buried, friends.

I shared my piece of earth
With young, but truly heroic men.
We shed our blood together,
And our wounds became our bond.
Blood was lost on foreign ground,
Three hundred thousand plus,
Yet history prints a single page.
No trumpets played and little praise.

They carved a list, a long gray wall.
The dead in silence stand.
Memories cut, in heartless stone,
By date, in numbered panes.
No peace decided by their deaths,
A country's wounds still linger on.
And you won't find a single man,
Who's laid to rest his grief.

After many years, a nation struggles,
To try to find the men it lost,
And bring them home; soothe the ache.
But years of pain, outweighs new honor,
Not easy to forget the hate and shame.
We suffered many wounds in battle,
Though the deepest one we keep;
Returning home, empty, greeted by defeat.

James M. Furber

Forever in his Heart

He is kneeling here, staring at you.
His strength would make you proud.
Unwavering, he watches you sleep,
Though he knows it's not to rest.

The sight of a child this young,
Paralyzed in a pose, unlikely,
That a boy his age should know.
He refuses to move from your side.

Songs play softly in the background,
Reminding us all of the mood,
And the reason for our gathering.
Your son remains fixed at his post.

Time passes quickly, the casket closes,
But the child is unwilling to let you go.
So hard to explain you have to leave.
Small hands touch you to say goodbye.

He stands and watches the casket lowered,
To somewhere he doesn't understand.
The eyes cry without reserve, yielding,
His mother buried, forever gone away.

A final resting place, forever in his heart.

James M. Furber

Cry Little Child

Cry little child. Your eyes so innocent and young
Should never have seen what has fallen upon them;
Such horror! Your delicate spirit overwhelmed by it all.

The look in your eyes, difficult to endure,
So terrified by what was there before you.
Brutal tragedy unjustly thrust upon your soul.

Step away from the visions now in your mind;
They will serve no purpose but to frighten.
Friends have come to comfort, the evil's gone.

The horrible deeds of this day will somehow pass.
Knowing no medicine will ever cure a wound so deep;
With hope and comfort we treat your weeping soul.

Come closer, rest now; think of your mother's smile.
She'd want you to leave here thinking not of her form
Or the way it is, but of her love, the way it was.

Sleep, oh dear savior of us all, have pity on your child

James M. Furber

The Confession

My brother, you're so saintly, but I fear you know not
Your life, a half century of pain and restriction
Days without family or love from your own
Imprisoned in places not dreamed of by us
You suffered from ignorance and public despair
Put away and ignored for your disfigured form
You prove more a man, than those who deserted

I hurt with an ache
That throbs deep within
I could give you my life
But it would never begin
To replace all the love
You've never enjoyed
And make up those years
Our neglect has destroyed

I come to you now and I pray not too late
I bring you my love in hope that I might
Bring comfort and joy the last days of your life
And help you forget the years you've endured
I've not appeared just to ask your forgiveness
Or bring you my pity for self satisfaction
I pray that your courage will help me be a man

James Hastings

The Poet

What driving force lies in a mortal's heart
To spur him to incant the magic of poetry?
How can simple words of creative thought
Put into print bring the sense of timeless life
And visions of worlds never known until read?

The poet is one such mortal soul with the written gift,
Engraving his eternal mark for lives yet unborn to see;
He takes the words and weaves a tapestry of vision—
It warms the searching heart with vivid metaphor,
Bringing to the surface a living, breathing, beautiful form.

The poet is a fowler and sets his nets with skill,
Laying down morsels of sweetness and bitter herbs–
The taste of which draws the reader into the trap,
And in the capturing, frees him to fly on new wings
That will ultimately coax him back to the gilded net.

The poetic heart separates a man from the masses
Yet drawing all souls to the cornucopia of his work;
In loneliness the art of verse is forged as a spark of life,
Fully nurtured by experience, time, and yes, even pain—
The poet truly sees each opus as his darling, daring child.

James Hastings

A Campfire Sonnet

Bright orange tongues leap from the crackling wood
As blinding smoke seeks my eyes from every angle.
Undaunted, I bask in the warmth of flame and embers,
Staring at the molten glow like a seduced moth.

Iridescent specks of brightness imbedded in velvet night
Have become my canopy over me and my campfire.
I look upwards, broken from the spell of the burning logs
As I watch a falling star race gloriously to its death.

An unseen legion of frogs unite in thunderous chorus,
Praising nature with their symphony of sound.
I feel elated by the raspy, croaking serenade
While I poke and prod the logs into fiery compliance.

The campfire is my focus, for its flame keeps darkness at bay;
Only shadows slip through this haven of burning light,
Dancing about like specters freed from their prison chains,
Fading quickly as the new wood catches and takes control.

As I prepare to rest in sleep, I let the faithful fire die out;
Night leans over, kisses and covers me with its blanket.
With heavy eyes that will soon close, I take a final glance–
The dimming brightness of the coals bids me a fond goodnight.

James Hastings

This Blessed Curse

Oh, this blessed curse of human life
That holds my soul within its grip
And leads me through the paths of time
Upon this world of pain and strife.

Yet joy and peace, their fruit I taste
As life has kissed with gentle lips
My face with love and tender care,
Giving me wisdom I shall not waste.

This outward shell does show its wear
For soon the dust will reclaim its prize,
But my soul within longs to be freed
When my flesh, it can no longer bear.

I have tasted both the bitter and sweet
That time has served and given me
Oh, this blessed curse of human life
It is you that has made my soul complete.

James Hastings

Very Little

Strange how though my eyes have seen millions,
A tidal flood of humanity passing through my life;
I only recollect what amounts to one mere drop.
Yet knowing you has filled me to overflowing.

I try to imagine every word spoken to me,
The countless discourses of fact and lore;
The total of what I retain embarrasses me.
Yet I hang on to every single word you say.

In love I have been with many other women,
Embracing the warmth and passions of them all;
Their names, in time, have sifted away like sand.
Yet it is your name, my dear, that I call at night.

Very little of what I have known remains with me,
Time and age has clouded so much of my past;
I feel sometimes that I remember nothing at all.
Yet your loveliness is all that I should ever know.

James Hastings

The Only Force No Man Can Tame

The angry rolls of thunderous clouds
Boiling with fury and ominous danger–
Each thrusts out hot, mighty spears of lightning
Burning the Earth with electric fire.

Rains of torrent slam the pavement
With hard, flood-like force as its intent–
Creating streams where none existed
And new channels that once were roads.

Legions of hailstones race from heaven,
Cracking glass and bending corn stalks–
Dancing so hard upon the rooftop
In machine gun tempo that overwhelms.

Winds pound the walls and beat on windows
As dark clouds take on the upward swirl–
And spiraling it consumes the dwelling,
Its vortex lashing with tornadic rage.

Great, roaring sounds of tempestuous nature
Have faded down to the gentle gust–
The rain, the clouds, the growling thunder,
It is the only force no man can tame.

James Hastings

Her Anniversary

Has it really been a year now
Since my world circled the sun,
Orbiting through the grief of time
With only memories of your life
That so quickly fade as my reward?

Has it really been a year now
Since I last felt your warm lips,
The mortal kiss of a final farewell,
Shared with the stains of both our tears
As your dimming eyes spoke of love?

Has it really been a year now
Since I walked into emptiness,
Hollow echoes of your laughter
Heard only with the ears of my heart,
And cried for the first time, alone?

I kneel by your stone and caress it
With a touch as gentle as the spring;
Cool breezes serenade with the leaves,
Playing melodies that only we two can hear—
Has it really been a year now?

James Hastings

Tell Me, Old Man

Tell me, old man, has age made you wise;
Are the deep wrinkles on your forehead
The worn road map of experience?

Is the thin, hoary hair on your head
The crown of longsuffering concern,
The burden on your shoulders fulfilled?

And your eyes, old man, they water so;
The light that sparkles tells mysteries–
Do the tears of the past still haunt you?

The rough leather that you wear as skin,
Does it remember the countless days
When sunlight burned and tanned years of toil?

Those old, tired feet, dear ancient one,
How many times have they shuffled by graves,
Bidding the rare, bosom friend goodbye?

My questions are all but foolishness;
Your toothless smile has answered them all.
I will hush, as we watch the sunset.

James Hastings

A Walk Through the Old Cemetery

I walk in the midst of monuments,
Arranged like a small community
Of stone and plastic flowers;
Each plot declares the name
Of some soul who had worn flesh
And life was his testimony.

I find the grave of a young child–
Intricate lambs decorate the stone;
Loving words inscribed in grief
Bid her a heartbroken farewell.
A fine layer of moss now grows
Where teardrops once had fallen.

I cast my gaze on a family plot,
Husband and wife side by side;
In life they loved, in death they lie
Nestled close and never to leave.
It seems to me that now they are one,
Entwined together in eternal sleep.

A simple stone marks a simple man
With only initials to regard his name;
No doubt poverty was his only friend
In a lifetime of toil and meager pay.
Unknown to me and nameless he lies,
Among the rich he has the same reward.

I walk slowly across this garden of souls
Planted along shades of maple and oak;
It seems as though each grave has its tale
Of a life lived and lost and soon to be
Forgotten until someone such as I
Touched their stone and lets them live again.

James Hastings

The Ballad of Charles Nobody

Old, brown shoes adorned with duct tape
Wrapped tightly around both tops and soles,
They have walked with me so many times now,
Taking the brunt of every callous, dusty mile.

My pants are khaki, but brown dirt hides the color;
A good washing would make them dissolve away.
Given to me with love from the homeless shelter,
God knows how many others have worn them before.

Torn shirt of red flannel, I wear in the summer,
Absorbing my sweat and the scent of cheap whiskey;
Both pockets collecting old cigarettes half smoked–
Why someone would waste them baffles my mind.

I curse my hunger and ignore it with liquor,
Perhaps someone will hand me a dollar or two;
A few days of famine, and begging comes easy
For I'm used to the stares and words of disdain.

I have found enough papers to make my bed chamber,
The ads of cars and restaurants mock me to sleep;
I dream of my past, yet in it there's no comfort,
Like hot, burning sand running all through my brain.

I suppose I will head on, out towards the river
And find some shade and rest for my soul;
Watching the barges and boats gives me pleasure—
Oh, what I would give just to sail far away!

James Hastings

The Changing of Tides on a Starry Night

The changing of tides on a starry night,
On a beach forgotten until daybreak,
Except by me; yes, I watch the swelling gulf
Whose waves capture the sea's bounty,
Proudly displaying its vast greatness,
Ignoring my meager existence;
Yet showing me its invisible power
To pull the waters unto its foamy bosom,
While drenching the crab's sand castles,
Depositing driftwood from long-departed trees
Which have sailed the oceans from unknown lands;
And to finally wash up and find rest alongside my feet.
At this, I marvel… Alone.

As the tide recedes and hurries home,
Under the countless eyes of Heaven,
Loosened from within the unseen grip
That had so omni potently held it fast,
I see to my amazement,
The adornment of shells
And of wood, and debris of man
Laced across the shimmering shore
As jewels of time and nature
Gently placed along the neckline of the sand.
And again, at this, I marvel… Alone.

With the changing of tides on a wondrous night,
Underneath the cosmic points of brightness,
I sense a feeling, no, a knowing
As immense as the sea itself,
Of the presence of One
Greater than myself and all the seas;
Greater than the sky and even Earth.

And once more, at this, I marvel…
I am not alone!

James Hastings

One Star

In moonless clarity I find that I have singled out one star
Chosen from the untold number of celestial embers;
Somehow it beckoned me and now my focus is captured
While I gaze upon the twinkling flashes of brilliance.

Of its given color I can choose my pick of the spectrum,
For it changes like a cosmic chameleon to suit itself;
Soft redness merging to a sharp blue, then fading to yellow,
Finding its whiteness briefly, then returning to the rainbow.

It seems that since there are so many, I should make it mine;
Would it be robbery to steal a drop of water from all the oceans?
I name the astral diamond after someone I loved long ago
And with a kiss upon my fingers, I christen my distant prize.

After some time I turn my gaze away from the lovely jewel,
And another one catches my eye and complete attention;
It occurs to me that perhaps my star had finished its course
And like my past love, its fire had gone out so long ago.

James Hastings

When I am But Ashes

In a sea of people I am but a drop;
An insignificant part of the complex whole,
Yet in myself, I sense a yearning to rise
Above the cold and faceless crowds.

Life is my art and my soul is the brush,
Painting the world with my abstract colors;
Obscure at first glance, the image matures
When one takes the time to stop and observe.

I am not pressed to conform to a life
That subdues me into some bland existence.
But I am free as a drop in the mighty sea,
An integral part of a great, swelling wave.

To leave my unique mark upon this orb
Before my last breath is taken from me,
It is my quest and my soul's desire
To be remembered when I am but ashes.

James Hastings

The Mountain's Call

Pressed hard against a mountain's face
Gazing at the foreboding summit,
With feet and fingers long since numb,
They coax and guide me toward my goal.

Cold wind cuts through every fiber,
Icy powder swirls white and blinding;
One more step and I take another,
Praying I will find safe footing there.

Casting aside all my pain and weakness,
A hand-hold has become my friend;
With borrowed strength I pull hard upwards,
And now I tread angels' hallowed land.

Only sky looms above me, cloudless,
I have left them floating far below;
Thin air revives me and I begin to ponder
As to what it was that drove me here.

The wind plays strange melodic music,
A gentle song of God and Earth;
This mountain now is alive within me
With the symphony that few have heard.

"Because it's there" is never the reason
as to why sane men risk their lives and toes;
But as we make our journey skyward,
We find that it is but the mountain's call.

Your Love

The sky in all its splendor,
Of its depth and untouchable size
Still is not the deepest place:
For deeper are your eyes.

The moon in all its grandeur,
Of its beatific grace
Still is not the most comely sight:
For more handsome is your face.

The ocean in all its mystery,
Of its secrets it strives to conceal
Still is not the most eluding thing:
For more baffling you make me feel.

The wind in all its softness,
Of its tame touch like a dove
Still is not the gentlest feeling:
For far gentler is your love.

Would You?

If the dreams of my fancy should take me far,
Would you walk beside me?

If the thoughts of fame should lead me astray,
Would you follow in my path?

If I were to change everything about me,
Would you still stay the same?

If I broke all my ties making myself free,
Would you ever call my name?

If the world accused me of wrongs I have done,
Would you come to defend me?

If people loved me, my name and my face.
Would you still remain humble?

If in prideful height, the world should shoot me down,
Would you be there to catch me?

Hannah Hastings

The Art of the Skies

The distant sounds of thunder
Echo through the night;
A sudden flash, a sudden crash,
Scatters all within its sight.

The sharp sting of the lightning,
Lights up the darkened skies;
In its fierceness, the sky it pierces,
Bringing fear to young one's eyes.

The growling of the thunder,
Its angry, desperate cries;
Raging wails, of its untold tales,
Now lost amidst the skies.

The thunder and the lightning,
The two will never part;
Now making haste, their hands embrace,
Touching Heaven's very heart.

The Prayer of a Child

Consider the voice of the songbird, my friend,
It's echoing voice so fair;
I thought it was the most graceful sound,
'till I heard a child in prayer.

Ponder the sight of the sunset, dear one,
Such colors of beauty so rare;
I thought it was the most majestic sight,
'till I saw a child in prayer.

Imagine the force of the storm, comrade,
It's strength I could not compare;
I thought it was the most powerful force,
'till I witnessed a child in prayer.

I thought of my life today, love,
Before I learned to care;
I thought that life was mine to live,
'till I was saved through a child in prayer.

C.J. Rider

Robert Lock

Mother, please don't cry for me

Mother please don't cry for me, for I have gone.
My pain's embrace has left, though *you* feel it still.
Turn your anguish to joy, for I am at peace.
In our trench's arms I lie; a sweet release.

And softly then the tender rain falls like blood,
Upon our upturned faces that see no more.
Lovingly sweeps the red mud from sightless eye,
With purest tears wrought from God's own summer sky.

And our trench fills with a profuse torrent then,
Carries remains of its hopeless protection.
Earthen walls, sandbags and bodies, everyone.
Seeks to escape the carnage we have become.

We're but empty vessels of our former selves,
The flow that seeks to wash away our remains,
Blushes as it turns an even redder hue.
Shamed witness of those, who know not what they do.

Mother, the foe were like us; all someone's child.
No malice in their hearts; there was none in ours.
Around their feet I beg you, let no blame, pool.
Cheap were our brief lives; sent here by those who rule.

We were as but leaves on a great tree grown old.
But as the leaves fall, so shall the strong oak too,
Weakened, helpless to stand against folly wind,
Roots consumed from within by men who have sinned.

Robert Lock

Mother, please don't cry for me (continued)

Leaders who knew the cost in our blood and lives,
At *their* spotless boots must all blame be now piled.
Vain, they called the piper, bade *us* pay the tune,
In granite should their shame be forever hewn.

So to grave we go; I hope for the best cause.

As symbols of the imprudence of conflict,
Peacefully safe with our friends, men, brave and true.
War that took so many…
                       Begun by so few.

The War Horse

He stamps, imprints iron-shod arc in hard ground
With hock, fetlock, drives hoof's timpani sound.

Great snorts gout from his nostrils wide and flared
Bellows vapor from pent up breath now aired.

Eyes wide and white, roll; expecting a "Charge!"
He snaps at neighbor, tries to trample, barge.

Reins are pulled tight, as the cruel bit takes hold
Prancing, mane tossing, he is ready, bold.

Curved sabers rattle as keen blades are drawn
Sparkle and flash in the weak sun of dawn.

See how dust rises from unfettered stride
As valiant six hundred start their last ride.

Then into death's valley, onward by league
Borne on brave horses, they now gather speed.

Deep thunder erupts from batteries lined
Cossacks and Russians crouch hidden behind.

Through volley and shell steadfastly they rode
Bravery, honor; two words of their code.

Charging into cannons, with sabers bared
Russian gunners slaughtered, none to be spared.

With just cut and thrust the Light Brigade fought
Bloodied, unbowed, the way back was then sought.

Out from the valley returned man and horse
But no more six hundred of that brave force.

Robert Lock

The War Horse (continued)

The whole world wondered over their foray
They are still wondering even today.

Time will not cause their proud glory to fade
All will remember the charge that they made.

He falters now, battle-weary and lame
Blood drips from chest, rider cries out his name.

To his knees the brave steed, drops with a sigh
Trooper sheds tears as he watches him die.

Last breath is taken and all now's at end
A man weeps farewell, to his faithful friend.

Robert Lock

My Few Words to You

When I was a young child I had a magic colouring book,
Its pages of uniformed grey and white awaited my trembling hand.
A scene of daffodils, marching in monochrome across a hillside
Would burst into yellow and green beneath my waterlogged brush.

Great swathes of drab sky would explode into deepest blue,
My young eyes widened in disbelief as the colours flowed.
Such is the wonder and innocence of childhood,
Beguiled by hidden pigments upon a page of mystery.

Now, in the evening of my life, the mystery and wonder of such things are one.
Colours that once were vivid and clear to me revert back to shades of grey.
Young eyes that sparkled in astonishment at the world, now water in sadness,
Not only for their lack of clarity, but also for what they *do* see.

Often, my thoughts dwell upon that book, its pages fresh and clear,
Existing now only in my mind, and perhaps also in yours,
And I ponder; will children of the future ever feel that wonderment?
Could such a *simple* thing ever bring pleasure to a child's heart again?

When I was a young child I had a magic colouring book,
Now in a world where indifference and apathy paint upon a canvas of neutrality,
I write these few words to you; from a pen dipped into the colours of my soul,
They fall upon the page, in my desire to bring a little rainbow into your life

Robert Lock

The Galleon

A sad silhouette beckons to me across the wind-swept beach
Carcass fingers that reach imploringly into a blue, cloudless sky
As if beseeching the saddened breeze to billow out sails long gone
Draw me close, as a voice born by the wind cries through barnacled ribs

The voice tells me of desolation, of loneliness, of despair
My hand runs reverently over sea-worn oak, crevassed and damp
Now home for the tiniest of sea creatures, protection until tide's return
And I speak to the wreck with the softest of words and recognize its pain

In mind's eye a proud galleon sails with white sails unfurled,
Foam racing from its bow as it dips and rises like a frolicking horse
Men, hard and sun-weathered, scurry to keep her running fast and free
Gnarled hands caress her wooden body with the love only a sailor would know

A gull's scream, echoes the tortured cry of her hull as she starts to founder
As a treacherous reef lays claim to the life of yet another fair sister of the foam
Captain shouts orders to head for the beach, and her heart of oak struggles to obey
On through the crashing waves she comes, her hull torn, her hurt reflected in her crew's eyes

Safely upon the sand she now rests, her final act done, her crew safe
The tide recedes; she settles lower into the greedy sand, timbers creak, spars crack
Nothing can save her now, and in final humiliation her body is stripped by scavengers
Four hundred years pass, she beckons, and I approach, my heart feels her hurt, and I cry too.

Robert Lock

Gelert's Return

Curse my anger for it was quick, my sword was even quicker,
when blood I spied upon your flank and o'er the baby's wicker.
Oh stabbing blade that found your heart containing but affection
be sheathed now in tearful sorrow and cast-off in sad reflection.

Now my turn is come oh faithful friend to join you in the chase.
For time has won the battle-royal and death has shown his face
I lie here as a child once more, too weak to raise a hand,
and dwell upon our hunting days when we two ruled the land.

No finer friend to Prince or man could I ask for or be given
and as I close my eyes, for the final sleep, I beg to be forgiven.
My son you saved, I knew it late, your bravery I did not discern.
'Twas not his blood, but the wolf you killed, too late I was to learn.

The years have past I bear them all, a weight upon my shoulders.
The heavier burden is within my heart, the shame forever smolders.
If only I had stayed my hand that drew your life that day
I'd welcome death contentedly and follow him on his way.

Oh Gelert! You come once more to my side, you lick my fevered brow.
Though night has fallen I feel you close, my soul is lightened now.
At peace, I may now seek to slumber, your head upon my chest,
and we'll hunt together once again, when I awaken from my rest.

Robert Lock

The Lonely Teddy Bear

A little Teddy with no eyes sat alone upon the toy store's shelf,
Covered in dust of years gone by, he was always by himself.
All other toys within the shop never stayed for very long,
Some visited for a little while, spoke to him, but soon were gone.

The Teddy couldn't even cry, though his heart was broke in two,
And as time ticked on with a leaden beat he didn't know what to do.
All his hope was lost, as on the shelf he sat, never to be bought,
Covered in dust and blinded, never given a second thought.

Then late one day the shop bell rang as the door let someone in,
Teddy sat up very straight, tried to smile, at least show a grin.
A little voice from far below said, "Daddy, that's the one."
But Daddy replied "It's broken though, it has no eyes my son."

"But that is why I love it. I want it Daddy, don't you see?
The Teddy has something wrong with it, has a 'problem' just like me."
The father sighed and kissed his son, "You are such a loving boy."
He paid the shopkeeper the asking price as he dusted off the toy.

The Teddy was overwhelmed with joy as in arms he was finally hugged,
No longer alone and upon a dusty shelf, now played with and happily tugged.
As the shopkeeper closed for the night he watched the trio depart,
A father crying happy tears for his crippled son and his loving heart.

An empty space upon his shelf made him look up to where Teddy had sat
"For everyone there is a place, even for a poor little bear like that."
As the sun waved goodbye to another day and night threw its cloak over all,
In a bedroom not too far away slept a boy in a Teddy's arms so small.

Robert Lock

Y Ddraig Goch (The Red Dragon)

Sweet beast upon our flag most proud,
We implore you, inflame us once again.
Though not just on this torn cloth.
But rise up from earth's damp grave;
smite our land's enemies with furious passion.

Fight with fire and flame, tooth and claw.
Write your vengeance from lofty clouds,
upon the hordes that invade our land.
Etch on them in burning letters your name.
Wait! Mountains rumble, ground cracks asunder.

Hark now! Do you stir?
Your banner swirls above my head.
And my grateful eyes weep unashamed,
in certain knowledge of your return.
Behold! Witness our ravagers recoil in mortal fear.

For our dragon surges from the earth once more.
Hungry for dreadful revenge;
Thirsting for the fray.
Look now! He rises! Great wings unfurl;
And he is of the deepest red, the color of blood!

Robert Lock

I am Moby Dick

I sound now, go deep; full ten fathoms under.
Your flailing stops, body chills as pressure bears.
Your fragile limbs rend as you wave a last goodbye,
My white hump, bearing your scars, carries you down.

The hunt is over and the hunter has lost.
Through oceans wide and deep we have danced.
Your hate driving frail wooden boats to my jaws,
As if you offered yourself and comrades to my wrath.

I did not seek you; nay you sought me.
Through my sea pastures, watery plains you came.
Pequod strove to undo me and for what?
Vengeance for a lost limb, oil for a guttering lamp?

Ahab, you and your kind do this world dishonor.
Thoughtless, you reap the seas as a rapist,
And we creatures of the green depths can but mourn.
But some, such as I, take bloody retribution.

Pray why did you burst your heart with hatred?
Must all Adam's sons pile their anger on our kind?
We pitiful few beg to understand your reason
You are King in your realm; must you be so in mine?

Others can only cry hauntingly for those already lost.
As white spume foamed with heart-torn red,
We watched them die, to feed your light.
Such is the shallowness of man.

But for you, Ahab, the dance is done.
Now my sea-dwellers will feast on your scant flesh,
And as the last of your crew strikes for land,
I breach; let him see his nemesis; I am Moby Dick, fear me!

The Little Geisha

Beneath a weeping willow she sits
A graceful study of perfection
As leaves shed tears of morning mist
Into a pool, casting her reflection

She had cried, had lamented once
Sitting in her Japanese Garden
The geisha stares with eyes unseeing
Thinks of loved ones, and prays for pardon

Her painted face, with cupid lips
Shows no sign of shame
For deep within her troubled heart
She knows she's not to blame

To love her master's only son
And have that amour returned
Was both heavenly and abhorrent
When her love was finally spurned

Now carrying his child within her
She sits alone, beneath the tree
And gazes deep within the pool
Sees the future that is to be

The scorn she'll bring upon her head
The hurt in her father's eyes
And for the last time in her sad, brief life
The little geisha cries

A folded napkin at her knees
She opens with shaking fingers
The blade beneath the linen flashes
And her gaze there fearfully lingers

Robert Lock

The Little Geisha (continued)

She grasps it quick while her strength is there
Her resolve is true, and sworn
And then holds the dagger to her breast
Above the heart so torn

A last goodbye she murmurs softly
To her garden in the glade
Then as if to sleep, she eases forward
To fall upon the blade

The little geisha finds her peace
Will never hear the word, 'harlot'
And the weeping willow drops its leaves
Into the pool of spreading scarlet.

Robert Lock

A Texan Iliad

"Remember The Alamo!" Three words cried with pride
Remember two hundred, who took refuge inside.
Brave men of many races who heard Texas call,
Rallied to the Alamo; defended the wall.

Santa Anna was slighted, could not let it lie,
And through his vain pride, over one thousand would die.
His fort had been taken by barely one hundred.
Across Rio Grande, his army now thundered.

The Siege of Bexar cost old Ben Milam his life,
But ignited a spark in Jim Bowie, the knife.
Crockett and Travis, names we'll always remember
Tejano, Texan, vowed — "Never surrender!"

In dawn's early light the final battle was fought,
Santa Anna attacked thrice. But all came to naught.
Then defenses were breached on his final assault,
As his men rampaged through, he would not call a halt.

Now no quarter was asked, and none would be given,
So Texans strove on, though their forces were driven.
Hand to hand they fought now, until all then was lost.
Freedom calls for a price; heroes won't shirk the cost.

As the sun rose that day, it must surely have wept,
Bearing witness to their cost. Of vows they had kept.
Davy Crockett and six, survived up to the end.
Execution was quick, death was welcomed as friend.

Daughters of the Republic! You Men of the West!
Fly your flag highest; see it above all the rest.
Smile; The Red, White and Blue now unfurls in the sun.
"Remember the Alamo!" The Liberty won.

Robert Lock

Soldier's Tears

The young boy lies cradled in my arms; dying
And I am lost for words.
His mother struggles, held back by my men; crying
And I am lost for words.

He stepped from the darkness, in his hand a gun.
My weapon silenced his outcry, it is done.
I wonder, did he think we'd come to enslave his nation?
As I kneel before him as if in supplication.

His young blood flows between my fingers,
Pained eyes find my face, and his gaze there lingers.
His mother screams as he sighs his last breath.
I close his eyes but I'll see them till my death.

We are only here with best intentions,
But not all agree with our interventions.
Then the gun I saw drops to the floor,
But it's not a gun, just a toy, no more.

And as a young boy lies cradled in my arms; I'm crying
And I am lost for words.
And as a mother struggles to reach where he is lying,
I am lost.

The Serpent Smile

Oh forbidden fruit of Adam's bane
I wonder if he knew your name.
Were you deepest red or green so pale
that cost mankind dear Eden's vale?

Was it with first bite he knew the end
we from God's garden he would rend?
Or did he consume it to the very core,
and in his ignorance crave for more?

And as Man and Woman left that place
ashamed to look in Michael's face.
Did the Serpent smile at his shameful deed,
and mark Man down as a thing of greed?

He had found the way to Man's temptation
that would cost a Son for our salvation.
And as the core fell from poor Adam's grasp
did he see the worm within at last?

Robert Lock

Father, Thank You

Father, thank You for this morning
For this little tree
Thank You for the shade
That it affords to me

Beneath it a stream meanders
Over weir it runs so swift
A salmon leaps in graceful joy
Its life, Your precious gift

Too many times we beg You
Request things that we most crave
But too little we acknowledge
How much we misbehave

Father, please forgive us, of
Our demands that cause You strife
Grant us the recognition
That allows You in our life

Though we see You in each detail
From every petal to every star
Clear our eyes from avarice
To see how fortunate we are

Your Son once walked among us
Returned to You on Calvary
As He died upon that brutal cross
To set us sinners free

Let us appreciate Your bounty
We accept without a thought
And praise Your gracious presence
For without You, we are but naught

Robert Lock

Follicly Challenged

This barren dome, damned cranium bare
That once so flowed with lustrous hair
You betray me with your flashing beam
That startles horses when I'm seen

Those lovely locks so careless shed
Found on my pillow and not on head
I mourned them all as their life did wane
And swirled round sink, disappeared down drain

"Comb over" I tried, to hide the loss
Made jokes of rolling stone and moss
But in my room I cried alone
When finally threw out my faithful comb

And shaved off the last few failing strands
That clung to scalp with desperate hands
Then heard the words I do most hate
As my daughter slapped my naked pate.

"Hi baldy!"

(Author's note: To all the curls I know)

Robert Lock

This Ring hath no Hand

This ring hath no end, no matter how you view,
The band round your finger that I gave to you.
This circle wrought from earth's a uric treasure,
A token of my love, too deep to measure.

You wear it now, as I do mine,
Symbols of our love sublime.
Two hearts enjoined, two pledges taken.
Two rings exchanged, two passions waken.

At last the kiss and the knot is sealed,
High in the tower the bells are pealed.
The deed is done we are bound for life,
You call me husband, I call you wife.

Time passes on, we watch it flow,
Ever hand in hand we see it go.
We raised our children as best we could,
Taught them to know the bad from good.

As one we traversed our lives together,
Knowing even love can't last forever.
'Till finally to earth return we must,
As ash to ash and dust to dust.

We passed through life in each other's care,
Laughed, wept and partook of life's great fayre.
Of us now you will never find,
Only two gold rings somehow entwined.

(Dedicated to my wife Anna)

C.J. Rider

Mark Manis

Rural Kentucky Morning

Mornings start early,
on the corner by the five and dime.
stirring the hearts of native born,
as young run along and play.

Old men in their faded overalls,
plant themselves on cedar benches.
From the maple sticks they whittle down,
old debates begin anew.

Gentle hills are nestled near,
above the country hollows.
Traditions live on in the distance,
teaching Appalachian ways.

Through the eyes of old and wise,
life's simplicity is cherished.
Folklore tales are handed down,
recalling the struggles of troubled times.

Mandolins and banjos create sounds,
stirring the hearts of native born.
Tying together both neighbors and kin,
in lively talk and common threads.

Past and present unite in one place,
timeless in beauty and stature.
Genuine in their customs and grounding,
content in their heritage.

Mark Manis

Another Life

I imagine another life,
a writer, a poet,
a young man who fills notebooks
with thoughts pouring from a subconscious waterfall.

The scribblings from crayon representations
of stick figure people with
vaguely detailed backgrounds
and wide smiley faces on a sunny day.

Through professors and partners,
the pictures take on a media transformation.
The crayon evolves into a colored pencil,
faces become distinct.

Months and years refine the pencil
into a paintbrush with a vast palette.
Words explode into vivid images
painting a canvas of crying faces
interspersed with portraits of joy.

I touch the minds of readers
with similes and metaphors
and with luck, I make them think
for a brief moment before they move on.

I draw with my words,
sketching a crayon self-portrait.
A middle-aged man with too much time
and an active imagination.

Mark Manis

Scarred

The shadows loom over my icy bed,
a checkered comforter envelops my body,
yet a blight darkens this heart.
Window blinds block out the golden rays,
determined to penetrate the black.
With thoughts of hopelessness,
I cover my head,
drifting.

Children ride their bikes,
their laughter torments me.
Forced into remembering my younger days,
the teasing echoes in my mind:
Chosen last in recess games,
never invited to sit,
left alone,
crying.

Time helped alleviate the mental wounds,
my mind focused on grown-up affairs.
Every day, I see a reminder,
as I drive past the playground.
An obese little boy sits alone;
the tormentors tease and taunt,
vocal knives carve his image,
scarred.

Mark Manis

HANDICAPPED

People stare
Looking in fear
Watching tragedy
Feeling pity
I try to ignore them
Seeing their expressions
Observing me
They're fortunate

I am wheeled
Demeaned by few
Rejected by many
Shunned by others
I speak so few words
Appearing to be dumb
They think I'm dense
They don't comprehend

I have a mind
Preparing actions
Processing ideas
Showing emotions
They're blind to my beauty
Deaf to my voice
Feeling pity
They're handicapped

Mark Manis

The Planting

On a clear cold day,
looking out into a desolate field,
decayed corn silks stand out
on a plane of dusted snow.
After the melting and
the return of the verdure,
nature's warmth loosens the ground,
welcoming spring's passage.

Turned soil of chocolate brown,
exposed to warm vernal air.
Garden tools form uniform rows,
combed and trimmed for presentation.
As the dark pink seeds go down,
I wonder what the yield will bring.
Covered with Earth's blanket,
growing season begins anew.

Mark Manis

A Kiss of Moonlight

Traveling along an empty road
with the spangles of stars and
moonshine as my guides, I
follow a lonely farm path,
seeking a repose from my
day-long journey.

On this plain of wheat, I
construct my nightly bed.
A tattered sleeping bag and
a soft feather pillow call me
to partake in midsummer sleep.

As my eyes begin to drift, I
notice a gossamer structure
in the distance.
Wind chimes fill my ears
like ruffling leaves, calling
my name to follow.

Barefoot and weary, I stumble
to this transparent place. A
woman of heavenly beauty
leans along a gauzy column;
with eyes of ocean aqua,
and a diamond stare, she peers
into mortals' guarded hearts.

With glittered sapphire hair,
she entices my longing for a touch.
Welcoming arms embrace my body,
as calm and contentment fill the
vacancy inside this frame.

Mark Manis

A Kiss of Moonlight (continued)

"Welcome," she says to me,
"you have been lonely a long time."
I try to utter a word, but
she gestures for silence.
"I am here for you now,
let your heart lift,
for I watch over you every night."

With lips of violet, she touches my face,
a calm settles over this soul.
A whisper trails in my ears,
"Luna is with you, remember always."
The night becomes a dream:
with hands embraced, we
drift through the celestial sky.

Waking up to the coming dawn,
my clenched fist reveals a gift.
The maiden's left part of herself
a strand of hair, a memento of our time
As the rays of light announce
the day, the structure fades once more
Our night is over, yet the bond remains,
eternal.

Mark Manis

Grief and Acceptance

The roar of the winds echoes my empty heart.
My soul dies as fall fades to winter.
My love is no more.

I pay my respects to my beloved.
He's moved on to eternal peace,
yet I remain, struggling to accept.

Once my spirit soared through temperate lands,
now replaced by a tundra of despair.
Why did you have to go?

My tears flow freely from my eyes,
I want to join you now,
yet I must remain on this world a while longer.

I shall accept your death my darling,
your spirit is free of this world,
part of you will stay with me,
until we're joined again.

The Dawning

Following the shadowy departure of night,
lightening the canvas of fusains
and chalk

hangs an atmospheric masterpiece,
dotted in cotton and spectrum
hues.

Stratus and cumulus blend in starlight,
layered into drifting figures
along the horizon.

The artist's creation incomplete,
evolving with each
infinite stroke.

Static and active at once,
a lazy river in the sky;
a visible alpha and omega,

floating above pedestrian viewers.
A moment of awakening,
switching on the first light,

existing for an
instant;
the miracle of dawn.

Mark Manis

Under Luna's Sky

Luna's rays kiss your auburn hair
as we stand along our back porch.
Your voice, quiet in the dusk,
whispers soothing words in humid air;
fanning the flames of passion that burn
inside this yearning body of mine.

Walking with you to the trees,
the spider shadows provide us shade.
Your fingers tighten in mine as
our lips touch softly at first, turning
into a soul kiss, wrapped in the
moist summer heat.

Dampened skin conquers,
once we shed our clothes,
Caressing hands wake my primal urges
as I take you down by the brush.
Ignoring the howls of night creatures,
I focus on your pleasing sighs.

We share the flood tide of ecstasy,
united in the intimacy of our bond.
Another soft kiss in our restful state,
as we admire the spangled sky.
We spoon in a tender cocoon,
admiring Luna in our afterglow.

Mark Manis

Barren Road of Enlightenment

Walking down a barren road,
alone in this desert wasteland,
the sky changes from bright to dusk,
as the ball of fire
gives way to a celestial curtain.

Crickets sing their song,
as wolves bay to the moonshine,
their spirits call out,
a gesture of invitation.

Something compels me onward,
what is it I can't perceive,
their song entices me,
urging me to continue forth.

Tribal drums grow closer,
what secret have I uncovered?
A woman appears,
a spirit with raven hair and
eyes of deep perception.

I feel I have known her
yet a stranger to my eyes.
Her arms spread open,
engaging me to join her.

Mark Manis

Under the Stars

The last rays flowed over wooded hills,
the auburn river blazed with light,
as the sun descended over the horizon.
Twilight aged slowly to violet,
sprinkled with sequined stars.
With the thought of relaxation,
we paddled to the muddy shore,
anticipating.

The campfire crackled, splinters curling orange,
foil-blanketed potatoes rested warm in their ember bed,
salmon spit in the smoke seasoned skillet,
gold butter slid underneath,
teasing me, taunting me, begging me to taste.
An explosion of flavor, toes curled in delight,
chewing until there's nothing left,
replete.

Above us the stars swung from invisible strings,
spangles dangled from heaven's mantle.
Insects kissed the flame beside us, daring
as a meteor flared its dying trail.
Preparing for bed, we bared ourselves,
the chill night slid over the fire's sandy grave.
Sharing the sleeping bag, we reached out,
consecrated.

Mark Manis

Another Morning

Ebony fills my windowsill,
the sun still a stranger.
Out the window crickets chirp
and the wind blows through leaf-barren branches.
Pale moonlight glows above,
reflecting the morning dew.
At the feeding tray,
cardinals eat remaining crumbs.

My butterscotch cat goes spread-eagled,
spotting the feather winged guests.
He invites them over for breakfast, yet
they refuse his overt offer.
Disappointed by their refusal,
he goes upstairs to ponder life,
even before the morning light, while
I drink my second mocha.

Mark Manis

Light Touch

Committed, I stay at her side.
Longing for her,
I beg for attention.

I am the light,
casting dusty rays,
shining through curtained rooms.

Her eyes open,
my warmth flows through her fingers,
her palm stretches, holding me.

She whispers, "*Dance*"
blowing soft chaos
into a concert of whirling dots.
Watching them waltz
into dark, distant places.

Mark Manis

Simple Pleasures

Rolling horizon
Dotted with green
Morning dew
Kissing sunlight
Cotton floating
Adrift in blue
Forming shapes
Open rendering

Walking barefoot
Cool relief
Refreshing air
Time to breathe
Simple pleasures
Invigorating moment
Relax and reflect
Enjoy life again

Mark Manis

Connections of Water

A single drop
fallen from the sky
splashing onto the ground
splitting into a multitude.

Water flowing
running down a stream
along fields and roads
racing towards the unknown.

A winding river
bordering opposing sides
different in name
common in ground.

An ocean adrift
forcing people apart
appearing to connect
divisive beneath.

C.J. Rider

James Oldfield

The Production Line

I picture men of noble blood,
Whose works before have caught my heart,
I see the knights of bad and good,
Who never seemed to stay apart.
I grasp for clues of how they'd think
And pray for words to paint their souls,
Then soon I have a place to start,
As from their lives I deem their goals.

A soldier caught in wars he hates,
Who dreams all night of peace for all,
Whose wisdom never penetrates
The lord who gives the battle call
I see his anguish chalked inside
And feel his pain in every fray,
So now I try to catch his gall,
Through tears I'd not felt yesterday.

His deepest fears are born from ink
As paper sheets produce a man,
And then I quest to see a link
Between my soul and fields he ran.
I wish to share for fleeting days
The way he viewed the world he knew,
To see just where his fear began,
So then to know the things he'd do.

Thus I write a being I'm not,
Yet somehow think I may yet be,
I wear, for times, the soldier's lot,
And act as if this man was me.
So in the end I simply write
The thoughts I feel within my head,
The flow of words being quick and free
As every other line I've said.

James Oldfield

The Muse

Goodbye sweet muse, the hour has come,
And we must part another time,
Without your words my pen is dumb,
I'll lose my rhythm and my rhyme.

For many years I took the praise
That songs of yours had gifted me,
Now other joys must fill my days,
As you, my friend, again are free.

So fly once more to other lands,
And learn of beauties never seen,
Whilst here I wait with silent hands,
Until you tell of where you've been.

And if no more I see you smile,
Then no more words I'll ever write,
For as you travel every mile
I lose the guidance of your light.

So come back soon to point my eye
To places it has never known,
As I again must say goodbye,
And face the world I love alone.

James Oldfield

Mr. Balloon

Banshee wails dismember joy,
And countless faces turn to see,
This stricken, flailing, little boy
Who clutches air where friend should be.

His face, plum red, is burnt with tears,
As if his eyes could slowly melt,
For nothing in his greatest fears
Can match the theft the air has dealt.

Now wounds are cast on blissful times,
And summer smiles are scraped away,
As winds are cursed for heinous crimes
That stole the joy from this child's day.

And though in time much more is lost,
Than left his side one distant June,
They'll never match the pain that cost
The smiling face of one balloon.

James Oldfield

The Door

A vast field greets my waking eyes,
Its contours soft and somehow clean,
Red roses grow beneath clear skies,
Before me lies my radiant Queen.

She smiles with warmth that fits the day
And clasps my hand within her own,
Yet as I stir from where I lay
I spot an object all alone.

A cast iron door is standing tall,
Amongst the plants and well trimmed grass,
And though it doesn't grace a wall,
Its lock is shut so none can pass.

We now both lie in perfect bliss,
Yet still the door burns on my soul,
And through each touch and tender kiss
My thoughts come back to that keyhole.

But am I vain to wish for things
Which frankly make no odds to me?
Or should the secrets each day brings,
If even small, be clear and free?

This empty torment racks my brain,
Though all else wears perfection's crown,
And when all other fears are slain,
It comes back still to pull me down.

In shame I keep these thoughts at bay,
I try to sleep and shun the fear,
Yet when I woke again today
A second door had spawned quite near.

James Oldfield

The Scythe

I trim the plains through night and day
As golden stalks bow in my wake,
I deftly clear the fields away,
Though cursed to never take a break.

My only friend shines ever bright,
A scythe so sharp it bisects stone,
Its blade the texture of moonlight,
Its shaft of polished human bone.

My reach is growing ever more,
As day by day I claim new fields,
And each one's broader than before,
As each one grants me greater yields.

Yet here I meet an unknown foe,
As now I gaze on something new,
Two trees grow strange to what I know,
Though standing tall as others do.

Yet these two live like none I've seen,
Their trunks entwined in snake-like guise,
Their plumes a single mass of green,
Bound as one before my eyes.

And in the leaves now high above,
A single bird sings out its bliss,
A white and glistening turtledove,
Born alone from nature's kiss.

And though the beauty be not matched,
I swing my blade with all my bent,
Yet still the tree is barely scratched,
And bears no mark of where it went.

James Oldfield

The Scythe (continued)

But more, the blade seems aged and dull,
Its moonlight surface no more clean,
And rust spreads out now to its full,
And robs it of its sharpened sheen.

In rage I land another blow,
Again the tree survives unharmed,
But now the age begins to show,
The wear from all the lands I've farmed.

The blade before of ageless steel
Now crumbles quickly into dust,
What once was smooth and cold to feel
Now lies alone in piles of rust.

And still I stare at unhurt trees
Their lives the end of all I've done,
And down I sink onto my knees
As tears of mine begin to run.

Never will my scythe come back,
But thus my curse is lifted free,
So off I toss my cloak of black,
And bear my face to all who'll see.

James Oldfield

Finity's End

Silence sweeps the summer sky,
No cloud nor bird the air offend,
And down below no car drives by
The house that rests at Finity's End.

For many years this world has stood,
Alone from those who claim to know.
A living being of stone and wood
Its garden-heart now free to grow.

The plants, it seems, bereft of care,
Have learned to rule the land they own,
And long the ground was never bare
As plant on plant has endless grown.

For years the beauty came in mass,
As colors merged from many bud.
Until, one year, from out of grass
A rose was born, its face of blood.

No one knew from whence it came,
No seed was known to touch the earth,
Yet through the garden spread its fame,
Perfection from a virgin birth.

For months it grew amongst the weeds
With, on its face, the mask of joy,
Until at last were sown the seeds
Of pains that would the rose destroy.

And all who saw it smiled in awe,
Though deep down mourned for days to come,
For under smiles were souls that bore
The truth that beauty's days were done.

James Oldfield

Finity's End (continued)

Brave the rose had no doubt been,
But foolish to have tried to live.
Its fledgling roots were young and lean,
And couldn't take all life could give.

Older seeds had claimed the ground,
And friendly roots starved newborn grace,
Until, at last, the rose was found
With mask of death now on its face.

The withered rose had dropped its head,
A year of smiles now seemed in vain.
Now lesser charms live on instead,
Beneath the falling summer rain.

The house itself was full of woe,
You no-where from the loss could hide,
And it was felt by none more so
Than by a man who lived inside.

Though free to grow the garden was,
This man had lived to share its whiles.
For beauty's only there because
It seeks to draw the viewer's smiles.

But smiles no more the man could find,
For beauty's death is beauty's end,
And so he set his troubled mind
To seek such help as he could lend.

The man was known by those who knew
To hold a flair for science's path,
And so he sought to give life new,
With logic, thought and careful math.

James Oldfield

Finity's End (continued)

He strove for days and shunned the rest,
But slowly hope began to fade,
For though he tried he never guessed
The rose could never be remade.

Outside the garden grew and grew,
Order lost without his eye,
Until at last he finally knew
That beauty was all doomed to die.

He placed the rose aside again
And cried alone for what was lost,
But rage now filled his aching brain
And revenge was vowed at any cost.

He couldn't help but place the blame,
And sought to let his anger sound.
So up he dragged his shaking frame
And burnt his garden to the ground.

He blamed the plants, who meant no ill,
But killed the rose without intent.
And blind with tears he went out still,
And onto them his rage was spent.

The garden burned throughout the night,
Many lives consumed as one,
And by the morning's faint new light
The man at last saw what he'd done.

His life's chief joy being lost so soon
He couldn't cope and lost his mind.
He let the rage he felt consume
All the joy he would ever find.

James Oldfield

Finity's End (continued)

Now the garden lay there bare,
A cloak of black its new found gown,
The mask the rose had come to wear,
High-fashion now throughout the town

In sorrow trudged the man indoors
And nursed the rose in cradled hand,
And out again the plant he bore
To join its kindred in the land.

A grave was dug where once it grew,
And in the rose was laid at last.
And back towards a world he knew,
A man of science scurried fast.

And now the house stands still alone,
Windows now being blackened out.
And no more's in the garden grown
To mask the ash that lays about.

Except, that is, a single rose,
Standing at the garden's core,
Its growth this time being unopposed,
Its beauty shining all the more.

But this time no one sees its face,
And no one to its needs will tend.
Alone it lives, in silent grace,
Alone it lives, at Finity's End.

James Oldfield

Yesterday's Tears

I reach for my soul,
Drawn on a page,
The thorns of the past,
Withered with age.
Black and white in black on white,
Tales of losses, songs of rage.

But all is not the way I thought,
As page on page no longer bears
The bitter scars of wars I'd fought,
Laments of old in tragic airs.

I start to read
Of pains that died,
But words are smeared
From tears long dried.
My pain by pain has been destroyed,
And now I'm free, my bonds untied.

In time the wounds indeed did heal,
As many friend had claimed they would,
And now I find I no more feel
As if I'm cursed, alone for good.

I see the world
I'd lost before,
And now there's hope
Behind each door.
And whilst the light has still not come,
My faith returns to rule once more.

For many years I only cried,
Now I waltz through ruined streets.
For when the tears of old have dried,
We're left with only empty sheets.

Eye Candy

James Oldfield

Samael

Blood has dried on heathen hands,
And now my time to fly has come,
From perfect bliss, to broken lands,
My sword unsheathed, my spirit numb.

They chose to blight the God I love,
Now I will show what curses are,
I'll rain down torment from above,
And watch them grovel from afar.

For years they'll curse the name I wear,
And hate the thought of deeds I do,
But they don't know the pain I bear,
My working day is *never* through.

For though I see them made to pay,
They never learn, and still they sin,
So I must fly out every day,
Most hated of the Seraphim.

They fail to see it's not my choice,
It's they who call on Heaven's wrath,
And I am slave unto His voice,
To smite them down the righteous path.

But still the blame won't lie with them,
They'll curse me like the fallen one,
They think no evil rests with men,
And never see the crimes they've done.

Now night has passed, my work complete,
And back I fly to rest once more,
As mourners rush into the street,
To praise the Lord they mocked before.

James Oldfield

Samael (continued)

They soon forget the ways they've paid,
For grievous wrongs against His name,
But still the calls for me are made,
Humanity, this angel's bane.

James Oldfield

The Hourglass

'Life's true worth' had read the case,
With eager hands I tore it wide,
But then confusion gripped my face,
A simple hourglass lurked inside.

I lolled it gently in my hands,
And found a letter laid below,
It read 'Your life is timed by sands,
Turn the glass and start the flow.'

Of course the sand began its fall
As soon as I had touched the glass,
I marveled now as grains so small,
Below were forming quite a mass.

Down I set the antique piece,
And gazed upon the growing mound,
But as I saw the pile increase,
I heard, behind, a sudden sound.

My door had locked without my will,
And I was trapped within these walls,
I shouted loud but even still,
I found no other heard my calls.

So back I went to sit alone,
The hourglass on my table now,
But deep inside me fear had grown,
And sweat befell my wrinkled brow.

Again there crept into my head,
The thought of words upon that note,
'Your life is timed by sands' it said,
And now a lump grew in my throat.

James Oldfield

The Hourglass (continued)

The sand was falling faster yet,
And now I feared my time had come,
I couldn't shake that written threat,
And wondered on what I had done.

In turning hence the little glass,
It seemed that I had sealed my doom,
And as I felt the moments pass,
My heart was overwhelmed with gloom.

Half the sand had come to rest,
And soon, it seemed, my life would stop,
Now all my days were manifest
In sand upon my tabletop.

But wait, I thought, what fool am I,
To think a letter seals my fate?
If some foul prankster says I'll die,
It doesn't mean the risk is great.

And so I sat and scorned the sands,
Now knowing they could do no harm,
I wiped the sweat from off my hands,
And pushed away that evil charm.

But sand still fell despite the scorn,
Of I who it had sought to scare,
But what if it was meant to warn?
And came to me from those who care?

I did not know the words were lies,
I did not know the words were true,
But still it sat before my eyes,
The curves of glass, sand ebbing through.

James Oldfield

The Hourglass (continued)

And now the time was running short,
As little still was left to fall,
And I still wondered if I'd bought
An evil scheme to end it all.

I could be safe, I could be slain,
But this was too much risk to face,
And so I turned the glass again,
And watched the sands fall into place.

Nothing happened, nothing stopped,
Least of all this heart of mine,
And back into my chair I flopped,
Content that I had bought more time.

But still the sands are seeping down,
And I am slave to turn the glass,
And I no more will see the town,
As still the door won't let me pass.

And all could end when sands run dry,
Release or death, I cannot know,
But I can't risk to move my eye,
From watching sand piles slowly grow

James Oldfield

Birdsong

Oh to know what dreams you sing,
To see the mind whose gossips bring
The birth of day from darkened skies,
And sing me home from first goodbyes.

Every day I'm drowned in words,
But none can match the morning bird's,
For meaning said cannot compare
To meaning felt through waking air.

For though the dawn awakes to gold,
The fledgling day is harsh and cold,
But warmth within me rises still,
As songs of yours fend off the chill.

So though I may not always know
The joys to which your warblings owe,
Always wear perfection's guise,
And sing me home from last goodbyes.

James Oldfield

Bliss

Dual sirens sing in cyclic wails
As steam seeps from an upturned car,
Sweeping like ghosts through rusted rails
Which mark the grounds of a downtown bar.

Amongst the plains of oil and glass,
Unholy seas snake through the land,
Bottled beer from a broken mass,
Mixed with blood from a now dead hand.

Yet life has not all left the scene,
A well-trimmed cat sips from the pool,
Its coat of white still neat and clean,
At home a house whose whims she'd rule.

Unaware of what has passed
She feeds her thirst without a care,
Until she's drunk her fill at last,
And licks the excess from her hair.

But things have changed for worse she finds
Her senses now seem warped and dull,
As beer that poisoned many minds
Now enters hers and starts to cull.

She wanders semi-blinded on
And props her form against a tree,
But all her sense of place has gone
And soon she finds she cannot see.

She hears quick movement all around,
Yet eyes of tears cannot explain,
So terrified she stands her ground,
And finds her body wrenched with pain.

James Oldfield

Bliss (continued)

She claws the air to no avail
In hope of striking who knows what,
But all her drunken efforts fail
As all her instincts now are shot.

A yelp of pain and all is dark,
Alone she dies from many cuts,
Above, two squirrels scale the bark,
Below, a worthless pile of nuts.

And all will mourn and days will pass
As children seek the pet they miss,
But none will find this gruesome mass,
With blood soaked collar, declaring 'Bliss'

James Oldfield

The Tiger

Noble feline, unsung king,
Nature's finest, greatest child,
I gaze upon your tempered sting,
Now you are hauled in from the wild.

You eat on call and sleep all day,
Your life is bound by human rules,
Yet how could it have come this way?
Has graceful might succumbed to fools?

In strength and speed your frame is best,
A man can't dream to match you there,
Your skills to hunt outshine the rest,
You've often caught us unaware.

Yet still it's you whose numbers fall,
And us who wipe you from your lands,
The Godly beast who ruled it all,
Now falls from grace to feeble hands.

So were we stronger in the end?
Could you not match the skills we'd learned?
Perhaps the strength our tools could lend,
Made up for gifts our species spurned?

Yet then the strongest seems to fail,
For you, no doubt, must wear that crown,
Yet things we'd made saw us prevail,
So was it they who brought you down?

Or were we blessed to rule the Earth,
To conquer all of every mould?
For thus, despite your noble birth,
In time your strength was doomed to fold.

James Oldfield

The Tiger (continued)

The only truth I seem to find
Is man alone would face defeat,
Thus you are King within my mind,
And either way we're nature's cheat.

But wait, one thought now solves my mood
The answer now is in my sight,
For whilst you'd only hunt for food,
We slew your kindred out of spite.

James Oldfield

The Samurai

I am slain.
Death's unearthly soldier has stolen from the night,
Dagger drawn, skin painted cold with morning dew.
He plunged deep into my heart, scar-less on my skin,
So now my world shall fade away and silence must begin.

So it ends.
A lifetime of honorable nothingness spent,
Alone I lie in every joy I have to show.
The deeds of my life, disappearing in the vault,
Five-score years of happiness and living without fault.

And my sword.
A gleaming rod of steel that lies by me at the end,
Sheathed again, for ever more, in studded leather robes.
Fury never held its hilt nor brought it down to rest,
And deathly beauty waits on now, forever ruby dressed.

As I doze.
But quick I wake to the rage of he who's wronged,
I see in an instant the injustice of my fate.
Death has shown no mercy, nor sought to fight me fair,
But only stolen from the weak, alone and unaware.

Death is a thief.
My life is a prize which he may never have,
He'd only waste, never feel the joys of its presence.
My sword wakes from thoughts of peace another time,
I'll not be slain by thoughtless hands, I'll rob him of his crime.

My death is my own.
The point of the blade nurses my heart, and I fall,
Ever down, towards the end I know I deserve.
The ghosts of my love surround my frame with their pride,
My blissful days now always safe and wrapped in joy inside.

My life was theirs.

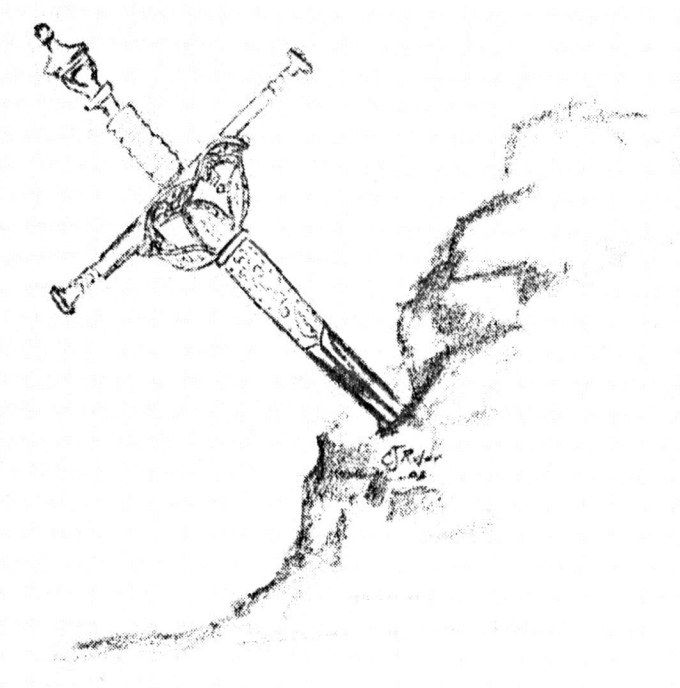

C.J. Rider

James Oldfield

The Shopping

It came one sunny afternoon,
The Parents brought ten pods of white,
They looked as if the distant moon,
Had fallen quickly from the night.

It seemed the pods controlled their minds,
As just like drones they did their will,
And peeled away the plastic binds,
To hide away their hidden fill.

I saw this action from my pen,
Evil acts through wooden bars,
And after talks with Teddy Ken,
We judged these beings had come from Mars.

Still we watched the Parents act,
As if their minds were not their own,
And then we made a fatal pact,
To guard the place where we had grown.

In time the pods were moved away,
And so the Parents left the room,
And we decided that today,
Would not be when we met our doom.

As plans were made in our defense,
I saw a sight that brought a tear,
Not three metres from my fence,
Another pod was lurking near.

The parents must have missed that one,
Or else it sat a silent spy,
Now what on Earth could we have done,
Within the gazes of its eye?

James Oldfield

The Shopping (continued)

And we decided there and then,
That we must stop this solo pod,
I searched within my small playpen,
But couldn't find a reaching rod.

But then my heart was filled with woe,
As Tiddles pranced into my sight,
And prodded round our deadly foe,
As if he planned to pick a fight.

Movement now and Tiddles ran,
The pod dispatched a Killer-Bot,
The small and shiny metal can,
Rolled towards my wooden cot.

This was it, they'd sent a means,
To kill us lest we told the rest,
As markings claimed they'd come from 'Beans',
And not from Mars as we had guessed.

I shut my eyes and bowed my head,
And waited for the end to come,
But then I woke up in my bed,
As if I'd dreamt of what I'd done.

Soon they'll put me in my pen,
And I must face the horrors there,
But now I mourn for Teddy Ken,
My brave but missing Teddy Bear.

Alexander Pavelich

Men of Greed

The Heroes came prepared for war
to take the fight to Evil's core,
with confidence in mind and might,
went bravely forward spreading light.

But light alone can't clear the path,
when suffers all a hellish wrath,
from deep below whence fires came,
still none above dare speak its name.

Its wings were large and fire burning,
Luck was there, but time was turning.
One of four had lost his knife,
the little flaw that cost his life.

The beast was slain and lying dead,
good had rid what evil bred,
Treasure lay there as their prize,
gold and gems in ev'ry size.

In glory slept the hero knights,
but knife to throat had shut the lights,
behind their eyes a simple deed,
Honor dead as killed by greed.

Together fight, together fall,
they pledged a vow agreed by all;
friends until the end of time,
none to do a single crime.

But heroes bold betrayed behind,
from friend made foe with gold in mind,
to take and plunder riches won,
t'was evil new, though old undone.

Alexander Pavelich

Men of Greed (continued)

One had vicious plans to do,
Deception was to guide him through,
he took the gold and killed the men,
none to see the two again.

Widows wept and orphans cried
as bards oft sang and maidens sighed,
for want of heroes lost below,
that haunt in sleep of ghostly glow.

Together fought, together fell,
'til good had won, though stories tell
the cursed tale of treachery,
when evil stole the victory.

Strong enough to break a pledge
alone with gold he stood the edge,
to leave his dungeon deed and hide,
alone he fell, alone he died.

Alexander Pavelich

I Fly

I fly, soaring over mountains high,
sovereign masters of the earth.
The clouds sweep gently by me,
as the soft breeze caresses my cheeks,
wind running through my feathered wings.
I see the green tints of wood and forest;
majestic trees roam over plains of grass and scrub,
Kings of all, beholders of wisdom.
Oceans of blue scintillate the reflections,
as the sun lights the Path only angels tread.

I gaze upon the sky at night,
a blanket woven by dreams.
It is filled with fallen tears of Heaven,
turned to the stars we admire,
wished upon, one and all.
The Moon shines in all its nobility,
our pathfinder, the guiding light of lost souls.
Rivers rush, carrying life and love to the sea,
soothing parched throats, begging us to stay.

The desert sands flash gold upon the Earth,
gleaming with purest light.
Masters of disguise,
blending in our minds, creating an image,
too beautiful for the eyes of man.
Above a world I wish could be eternal,

I fly, basking in its elegance.

From the skies as if made for us,
Like pre-made heaven,
Yarns of everlasting dreams spin around this jewel, our world, your home.

Alexander Pavelich

The Bard

I am the Bard that sings aloud,
and entertains the city's crowd,
with songs that are of joy and fun,
sitting under the shining sun.

I try my best to do them right,
and please the crowd before my flight.
Off I go, o'er mountains high,
From town to town, my time is nigh!

'Tis a craving task, to find the text.
I don't quite know what words come next
to suit my song of merry times;
It's difficult to fit the rhymes.

Before the day I go on stage,
I'll learn my lyrics, page by page.
There isn't time for a nervous mind,
no flaws of any other kind!

If one mistake comes through my song,
I'll have to play and move along,
For if I stop my merry tune,
My arse'll be whipped, that afternoon.

They kill, you know, if things go wrong,
for just a little, stupid song.
That's why I fall on knees and pray,
To stay alive for one more day.

The show is near, I hear the crowd,
Soon it's time to sing aloud.
With songs that are of joy and fun,
Another show has just begun.

Alexander Pavelich

Heart of the Forest

The heart of forest lies me near,
Between the woods and frozen pond
In darkest evening of the year,
I walk the path and far beyond.

Through mist and fog I find my way,
Never strayed and never lost.
I fear not night nor do I day,
I rule the flame, I rule the frost.

I will with my darling be,
For it is kept away from you.
Always hidden and safe with me,
no harm to it I'll let you do.

Be you friend or be you foe,
None else than me will it obey.
I'll take you deep, deep down below.
My heart will never go away.

The heart of forest lies me near,
Between my heart and clouded mind,
No evil thought will wipe it clear,
For there exists no other kind.

Cynthia Jeanne Rider

Begin Anew

Canvas placed on easel's ledge.
Long-stemmed brushes in a jar.
Camel hair for wispy sky.
Pig bristle for the stippled grass.

Tubes of color wait in turn.
Squeezed, one by one, they slowly ooze.
Gleaming softly, wet and daring.
In rainbow order, they lay complete.

I nip my cuticles, resting chin in hand.
Nascence, paralyzed. Emotion, restrained.
Pure white canvas, empty and cold,
Awaiting my brush, laden with hue.

Dabbling on in desperation.
Meaningless grume on pure white ground.
Blank canvas glowing, mocking my invention.
Picture hiding from mind's eye.

Ideas, tho' gradual, do come clear.
Brush in hand, dipped into paint.
Carmine Red, Indigo Blue.
Promising to blend, opus begun.

When my torment attains its peak,
My mind and hand become as one.
Holding brush as magic wand,
Dipping and dabbing, scene emerging.

I have conquered canvas once again.
First glaring and white under my hand.
Feelings of desperation, now familiar friends.
It begins anew with each creation.

Cynthia Jeanne Rider

Secret Garden

Hidden deep within my mind,
Exists behind a strong hedge copse
Where enchanting Erigeron flourish and grow.

Amongst the privet, the climbing rose
Intricately woven spiring wall.
Full of blooms and winding stems
Deceiving, with its jagged thorns.

A maze-like path leads to the heart
Where earth is smiling flowers galore.
Please push on, you soon will view
This rare and stunning scene.

Walls of rose-thicket line the lane
To ward off pests and prying eyes.
With a twist and turn, the path soon ends,
Displaying the gleaming jewels within.

The path breaks open to behold
The glorious inner sanctum.
Stand before it, not breaking the silence-
In awe of what you see.

Follow the cobbles around the beds,
Smell the lively, velvety scent
Of Angel's Trumpet double blooms,
Flanked along the walk.

Sniff the fresh odor of dampened earth,
See new sprouts bursting forth.
Calla lilies in the shade
Will take your breath away.

Cynthia Jeanne Rider

Secret Garden (continued)

Off the path, on heather-blue grass,
Kick off your shoes and wiggle your toes.
Soft and moist, it makes you laugh and
Forget all passing grief.

Pick up the trowel, turn the earth,
Nurture it for the next in need.
This special garden has magical power
To calm and center a troubled life.

Protect this secret and guard it well,
To keep the sanctity of quiet haven,
Lest throngs of feet invade its space
And wipe away earth's smile.

Cynthia Jeanne Rider

Secrets Locked Inside

Tall aspiring Saguaro,
Under the desert blue.
Reaching for the heavens,
Its secrets locked inside.

Stickling me endlessly,
Like a recurring dream.
As the soot within the night,
Its nectar cached above.

If only I could climb to see,
What the future portends.
Past events have left their scars,
For me to reason why.

Standing in the scorching sun,
My path unclear, yet firm.
Striving for the golden ring,
Sweat roiling on my brow.

I must reach the withered flower
And eat the plump red fruit.
For this is where the truth resides
In knowledge of the old.

Cynthia Jeanne Rider

Queen Anne's Lace

My garden is such a wondrous place
Of fragrance, gentle on the wind.
Drifting out into the world,
Beckoning all to come inside.

At blush of dawn the night awakes,
Sweet scents play on morning breeze.
Flowers open and seedlings grow,
Replenishing earth for all to behold.

New blooms revel in their short span,
Creating one ambrosial hand.
A Broad-tailed Hummingbird passes by
To sip sweet nectar through his nib.

Blue orchids ooze an ample goo,
For bees who make instinctive dives,
Collecting pollen on their way
To feed upon the bounteous flow.

While butterflies with wings of golden
Highlights fly across the sky
And settle upon a plant by chance,
To taste sweet life in Blue Bell blooms.

My garden exudes a silent beckon,
Attracting beasts to sumptuous feasts,
On bounteous treasures found so deep
Inside the iris standing tall.

Queen Anne's Lace is strewn about,
Large filigree tops abound in full.
They gather by the narrow walk,
In welcome to all that happen by.

Cynthia Jeanne Rider

Gecko's Tale

Soft, warm, gecko, hanging on the desert wall.
In a frieze of brown and gold,
Clinging tightly to the stone.
Thinking you are unseen
As you laze in summer sun.

The heat is so intense
You have to raise one foot.
Still not cool enough,
Slowly exchanging it for another,
To keep the timed dance going.

Across the great expanse
Time goes on forever.
Mirages of water and cities,
Make you right at home,
When indeed, you're all alone.

***

The hungry hawk flies in the sky
Riding currents high above.
Circling 'round on his last pass,
About to glide along his way
To the cliffs and cooling crags.

Then he spots your subtle shifting
To dissipate the heat.
Swooping in a hastened dive
Aimed to where you hide, in
Open view so none can see.

Cynthia Jeanne Rider

Gecko's Tale (continued)

Small feet release their hold
You fall to the sandy floor
And scurry into a crack.
Foiling this birds attempt
To dine on you today.

As the circling hawk goes seeking,
The cycle of life continues
Under a scorching desert sun.
Another chance is all he asks,
Just leave the rest to him.

Cynthia Jeanne Rider

Golden Embers

Childhood sweethearts stood
Before an outstretched life
Uncertain future looming
They stepped up to make a vow

Love flowed out with passion
For each other and one life
Pressed with expectation
Of time within the night

Days passed by unnoticed
Weeks slipped into years
Golden embers burning
Quiet love content

Completeness of a life now spanned
Your love runs deep beneath
More than just a lover
A protector of my soul

The softness of your touch
When I have fallen down
The sweetness of your breath
Whispered on my worried brow

These things are now remembered
When all has turned to gray
Loving you forever
Beyond the dawn of time

Cynthia Jeanne Rider

Tending My Garden

In my garden of golds and blues,
I lovingly toil with muck on my shoes.
I pull the weed that would strangle out,
The tender shoots beginning to sprout.

Bees buzzing gaily, to and fro,
Carrying the pollen that makes seeds grow.
Butterflies float gently from stem to stem,
Drinking the nectar within the gem.

The joy that it brings is beyond compare,
Tending my garden, with loving care.
Peace and quiet settles around,
When I practice to nurture, my blooms abound.

And, like a child, I laugh with glee
As I sprinkle the water on my brand new tree.
Making its branches grow wide and strong,
Tending the garden is my soul's sweet song.

Photo by C.J. Rider

Cynthia Jeanne Rider

Life Long Friend

I buried a life-long friend today,
Out in the meadow where he would romp.
Playing our games just to please,
Looking up to see my smile,
Then off he'd run to catch the wind.

Yesterday, we played bouncy-ball,
Scrambling across the linoleum floor.
Laughter and gaiety ringing true,
In reckless abandon to snatch up
The sloppy round object of our joy.

Playing the game until I would tire,
He would lap up water and feign interest for more.
Pushing his wet muzzle into my hand,
Soppy ball in mouth, he would beg
For one more quick toss, the ritual we'd made.

In the afternoons, we would play in the meadow.
This was his favorite, running free in the grass.
The bouncy-ball was part of it, too.
Carried in his mouth until it was right,
He'd flip it to me, slobbers and all.

As the years went by, we continued our sport.
Same routine day after day.
Ball in mouth, he would come to me.
Fun- not in possession, but in the pursuit.
Grappling and tossing and running amuck,
Always coming back, with the well-worn ball.

Pain filled my being when I awoke this day,
No wagging tail, no licking me about my face.
When he didn't come running, I called out his name.
I searched through the house, with fear in my heart.
There he lay, still- ball by his side.
My old life-long friend passed on in the night.

C.J. Rider

Cynthia Jeanne Rider

A Lonely Road

Sitting softly in the sunroom,
Withered features, half-erased.
While thoughts of where you've been,
Retrace the line of time.
Life can never be undone-
Regrets still haunt your mind.

Searching. Not for the carnal,
Hope soon drifts away.
Looking deep and longing
For the simple place within.
Meanings became commonplace,
You ignored the outward signs.

Desiring to dine alone,
Yet fearing what you'll find.
Who will be there waiting
When your final breath is drawn?
Tattered pieces left to fall,
Along Death's lonely road.

Cynthia Jeanne Rider

Golden Sweater

Blossoming young girl in woeful days
When ideas were ended before they began.
Rounding up neighbors and relatives alike,
Some went into hiding, this became her life.

Hiding and sneaking, when there should be joy,
Quietly quivering in fear's deathly smell.
Huddled together, with her mother so close,
A young girl grows up in silence and dread.

A bang on the door, men bursting inside,
They grab her small arms to bind them behind.
Shouting and yelling, they take them outside
To a car full of others, fearing their fate.

Driven through the country in the silence of prayer
Asking God to deliver them from what lies ahead,
They arrive at the station and are shoved on the train.
The young girl holds fast to her mother's moist hand.

Cynthia Jeanne Rider

Double Delight

The gardener loves to take a stroll
Amongst the flowers he doth grow.
Admiring each and every one,
Sweet, shining splendors, in the sun.

Searching out his one prized bud,
To prune and preen so it will burst.
Down the cobbled path, he trod
Amidst the green dew-moistened sod.

His route is not an easy one,
Bruising stones push on his sole.
Clinging thorns extract demands,
The bouquet awaits his gentle hands.

Radiant within a sea of green,
Double Delight top stems supreme.
The gardener needs to crop the bloom
To give the plant its growing room.

Onerous choice, he makes a snip.
Its soft head topples to the ground-
But not to ruin, it still has use,
Sitting pretty on chocolate mousse

Cynthia Jeanne Rider

Evening Sky

Some would say a common view,
The sunset flowering toward the west
Chased by darkness in descent,
One final trial of will.

In a fever of ribboned hues,
The ballet of light begins.
Carefully choreographed,
By some skilled hand.

Heads of gold, with tails of smoke,
As if giant meteors swooshed,
Leaving bold marks across the sky,
In constant contrast to the sensible horizon.

The wan of daylight and pale darkness merge,
Forming transparent shades of gray and mauve.
The meadow lark sings from atop his tree,
Trimmed in the last rays of golden sun.

The sighing wind breathes good eve
To the blossoms closing tight for sleep.
Galaxies of timeless stars
Shine in defiance of the night.

The moon illumes the evening sky
With wisdom, transcending time
And permanence of transition
In a work to nourish all mankind.

Cynthia Jeanne Rider

Virtuosity

With metronomic regularity,
Life revolved around the sound
Of my bow pulling across each string.
Soft and long till each note sang round,
With the reverb of a fine bell's ring.

Ardent lessons since gone by,
I practiced without rest,
As my fingers moved fine and true.
I attended concerts to hear the best
Snatch virtuosity from the blue.

If I could only play like them,
I simmered in my ambition.
Finally the call to play the part,
I'd waited for, came to fruition.
- Dare I display my heart? -

My good fortune close afoot,
Plunged me into a turmoil
Of misgiving and self-doubt.
I begged the courage to break this foil
Yet afraid to find what I'm about.

But alas, I crossed the stage that day,
Feeling my fingertip scars.
In formal dress without ado
I took my place among the stars,
Grasping virtuosity from the blue.

Cynthia Jeanne Rider

Spring Whimsy

Winter wakes for springtime view,
Sprouts break ground, sweet and fair.
Leafy packages, filled with hue-
Enshrouded- they wait, to perfume the air.

Twinkle toes and Geraniums line the walk.
Bees drone about, waiting to be fed
As a flower bursts open atop its stalk,
Exuding sweet nectar from its head.

A hummingbird swoops, twittering his song,
Seeking a trumpet to slake his thirst.
Drinking its sweetness, he won't stay long,
He flits from blooms to taste their first.

The scene is like a painting done,
Abundant colors edge the street.
Petaled faces turned to sun,
Releasing scent, so soft and sweet.

Cynthia Jeanne Rider

Taste The Sky

Man has no time to weep for the king,
His only task, to remove the ring.
Wallowing in riches, with one last breath,
The moment seized to grasp a wreath.

Silver coins, but now you're old,
Across the ages; forever told
Of timeless err- without end,
Where countless others learn to begin.

The cycle of life is on the rise,
Swift angel wings, the spirit flies.
Soft breath of gold, they speak in hues,
Of untold riches found in youth.

A time for those who promise to dare
And live a life of beauty with flare
Or leave it alone to wither in mask
Denying desire to taste the sky.

C.J. Rider

Lorraine R. Sautner

Outpouring

I am a fountain flawed
Pouring forth Your Love.
Shimmering drops of mercy,
Crystalline tears of compassion
Overspill, tumble from my Foundation.

I am merely an atomizer,
A struggling conduit of Your Spirit,
Not worthy of drying the Feet
Which carry me, nor the Hands
Which lift me. Selah.

My heart is a cracked cistern
Drawing from Grace, yet retaining
Little from abundance offered.
If from modest reservoir I partake,
Consider truly the vastness of its Source.

Lorraine R. Sautner

The Alchemist

If accountancy were a dark art,
he'd be a High Priest,
cloaked in deductible
interest income, conjuring
diabolical formulas of amortization,
and whispering incantations
in praise of the unholy
power of compound
interest.

"Abracadabra," he whispers
smugly from within the
walls of his Enchanted
cubicle. "For lack of verification
nations have crumbled and
rulers have fallen upon their
swords."

Sighing heavily, he
closes his eyes, feeling
acutely the burden of his
legerdemain, his exacting Craft.
"Fools!" he hisses, incensed.
"They heed not my prophesies!
Each goes his own way,
seduced by illusion."

Staring intently,
he stabs at computer keys
in a frenzy of numerical
alchemy and a trance of
long-division.

The Alchemist (continued)

"It is finished," he sighs
dramatically, resting his head
on his fingertips. "I have exorcised
the demons, conquered the spirit
of inaccuracy. The realm is safe
once again."

In a state of near exhaustion
and with trembling digits, he
raises to the heavens
his financial masterpiece,
lit from within by a supernatural
actuarial luminescence.
And in a final gesture of renunciation,
gently surrenders it to his Outbox.

…the expense reports are now completed.

Lorraine R. Sautner

Bird of Jove

When you can see beyond morning's horizon,
When you can dream beyond yesterday's end,
You will fly, blessed among eagles,
You will soar in faith again.

When ships set sail upon the ocean,
When souls digress in paths uncharted,
Hearts can break in tempest's raging,
Hope can heal in storms departed.

I know the Lord will keep His promise:
Your strength, He will renew.
You'll mount up on wings like eagles,
His love supporting you.

Life's journey is never forthright,
Perfection never without travail,
If we walk with wise men, we'll be wise,
Upon my friendship, you can prevail.

Lorraine R. Sautner

Sanctum Sanctorum

Follow me.
Take my hand and we can…fly
Oblivion,
never as sweet,
Transcendence,
never as fragile
as our holy freefall,
our esoteric shrug of surrender
into the shelter of Sanctum Sanctorum
…halfway between home and eternity.

Your question? Bring it.
I know the place where wonder is created.
Knock,
and the door will open.
Ask,
and you'll receive, wholly.
Your bittersweet redemption
eclipsed only by the anguish
of your prolonged
confinement.

Hope with me.
Let me show you, tenderly,
how shadows are illuminated
and treachery is forgotten.
Behold, again, the brilliance of a soul
as murkiness recedes,
as despair unravels.
The human condition reversing,
trembling as it yields to the embrace
of a sacred Valhalla.

Lorraine R. Sautner

The Prayer

I said a prayer for you tonight.
And doing so, released into obscurity
a fragile plea, a tiny pinpoint of grace
however small, fashioned tenuously
and set afloat in gossamer song,
heard only by those pure of heart
whose destination we could only imagine
as we watched their ships
launch from our shore
and whispered to ourselves, *Farewell,*
knowing we would meet again
in celestial time,
in a place whose beauty
would only break our hearts
if we could see it now.

I said a prayer for you tonight.
And doing so, sent into the breach
a desideratum, a timid firefly of hope
whose twinkling light
at first seemed pale, hesitant
as he ventured forth into uncertainty
from tarnished origin,
yet gaining speed
and brilliance as he found his
natural medium, soaring
trade winds infused with divinity,
joining his brethren in a borealis
of supplication, a waltz designed
to move the Heart of God.

Lorraine R. Sautner

The Prayer (continued)

Yes, I said a prayer for you tonight,
in fervent tone with earnest wish
to reach you, however far away
you sit, in whatever words
you use to beg release from sorrow,
I will speak them, with you.
My heart a stalwart butterfly
clinging stubbornly to faith,
in solace as you brave your tempest,
together as we entreat the Sun.

Jennifer Penix-Taylor

A Goddess' Quandary

My gods how my fate is terribly foul!
Athena is attended by a wise owl.
While I am accompanied by a rank swine,
who was once a lustful lover of mine.

How did he come to this horrible form?
He was unfaithful so him I did transform.
An error made, for now he is chained to me.
Alas with me forever he shall be.

Shackled here to my side forevermore,
No one knows how I suffer, bound to this boar.
Am I not also a most beauteous one?
Why then am I always to be outdone?

But wait, am I not known for my malice?
Tender roast pork with red wine in my chalice.
Perhaps a nice dinner is just what I need.
Yes, he will taste fine seasoned in dill weed.

Jennifer Penix-Taylor

Alone

I have no choice but to sit and stare,
For there is no one with whom to share,
The secret shadows only I see.
Send chills down my spine, I want to flee.

Ghostly voices near to me whisper,
Close my eyes, and try not to whimper.
Through my own thirst, I brought this about.
I unsealed the gate, I let them out.

Hidden Knowledge, was the thing I sought,
I opened that door, now I am caught.
Old secrets long lost, drive me insane,
And I have no one to share my pain.

Never seek what you don't understand,
Sanity fades; your soul wears a brand.
Life as I knew it is gone and dead.
Replaced by the visions that I dread.

Insane or psychic, which one is worse?
To me either option seems like a curse.
People will tease and people will taunt,
But gladly pay you when its ghosts they want.

It is a burden, I dare not share.
Who would believe me, could any dare?
If they did, would they be crazy too,
Or would that prove that my fears are true?

Jennifer Penix-Taylor

Alone (continued)

Cool numbness ebbs and flows through my veins,
I'm tempted to stay on the astral plane.
Into the matrix I have entered,
Only to find my perception splintered.

In spirit I am here, I am there,
Am I really anywhere?
Spinning, whirling, in my reality,
Can I not ignore them and just be?

Jennifer Penix-Taylor

Silent Beauty

Black shadows slowly creep inside my heart;
The seed of fear silently plays its part.
The pain grows deeper every darkened day;
I have lost all words which I could say.

Drifting apart, his love I need,
He will never see the tears I bleed.
Love is like a double-edged blade,
It causes pain that will never fade.

Some say words hurt less than deeds,
But I know well the hate they breed.
Day by day I watch them grow,
Too blinded by my pain to know,

That I do not deserve his taunts.
Like a ghost his cruelty haunts,
And the beautiful rose that was me,
Fades, leaving only a thorn to see.

Like that thorn that leaves a bloody stain,
His words pierce my soul, causing pain.
They twist and slash, never missing their mark,
As he leaves beauty silent in the dark.

Jennifer Penix-Taylor

The Seduction of Eve

Though you may see evil in my eyes.
I am eternally humble, genteel, and wise.
Be my protector and I'll be your twin.
Can you not be fond of a creature of sin?

You've only one thing to answer me.
I am here for you, are you here for me?
I am singing a song with a voice so deep.
These are my words for your heart to keep.

Just reach out to me and take my hand.
And I'll lead you to the Promised Land.
You will suffer without me if we part,
And feel my flames as they burn your heart.

Why do you not honestly believe,
It is you who I would not deceive.
Now take my hand and grip it tight,
For you, I will make all things right.

Jennifer Penix-Taylor

War's Mistress

The gates are open to await my love.
Sweet, gentle dawn arrives quietly,
Bringing blessings from Heavenly angels.
While the sun shines down upon me brightly.

So lonely have I been without him here,
Nights cold and desolate, missing his touch.
My river of tears swelling to the brink.
Too often gone, yet I love him so much.

Wielding a blade, I prefer to waiting.
I dream of him letting me join his war,
Nothing to do but haunt its passageways.
Confined to this castle that I deplore,

Embroidery does not absorb my musings.
Nor does any other feminine pleasure.
Why must he insist on shielding me from harm?
Afraid to lose me, his most priceless treasure.

We made passionate love on the morn' he set out.
He loathed releasing me before he departed.
"These foes are not simply beaten", he said to me.
What was this, my warrior is never fainthearted!

That fear in his heart, never present before,
Chilled my very soul, yet I had to be bold.
Memories flooded my mind of when we met.
When I first viewed him I had thought him cold.

He had waged a war against my people.
Facing my wrath, he acquired my heart.
Never before had I been beaten.
An' since that time we are loathe to part.

Jennifer Penix-Taylor

War's Mistress (continued)

Understanding, dawning, I emitted a sob
Never before had he forbade me from his side.
This time was different, his foes as strong as he.
An' he beat me when I was my finest, I cried

I had been angry with him for thinking me frail,
Never giving a thought that 'tis him I might lose.
He ne'er thought me weak, but the enemy stronger.
An' me a weapon they would have been sure to use.

If they are his equals, I did not stand a chance.
His common sense over his passion did prevail.
Realizing that which I was too proud to declare,
I would have died. Freya, I gasped, my skin turned pale.

Is it possible that he had felt it?
In his wisdom had he already known?
His royal succession assured in me.
For that morn' he left, his seed had been sown.

Will today be the day, that he comes home to me?
Have our enemies won, I won't even think it!
I am now war's mistress an' my hope never fades,
To hopelessness and defeat, I will not submit!

Sherri A. Tillman

The Connoisseur

Such a connoisseur
of fine wine you are.
Finding pleasure poured in minute
increments as a fluid eddy
in a taster's goblet.

I observe as you
place the bowl beneath
fine, chiseled nostrils.
Watch you savor aromas,
heady perfumes that give pause.

Your well-carved hand
cradling smooth stem.
I gaze as wrist slowly swirls,
shiver as your supple,
silken tongue extends.

The aromatic space between
wine and its searching tip.
You dip into the wetness
each taste bud aroused,
awakened to the bouquet.

Corked, keggy, wooded moss,
herbal undertone hints.
Florals, petals blend
on whetted palette to join
peppery tinges and exotic spice.

Sherri A. Tillman

The Connoisseur (continued)

Proclivity as innuendo,
a sensual inference
to more hidden appetites
whose subtle suggestions
draw my eye with delight.

You discern so, my love.
I watch each nuance, breathless.
Eyes heavy lidded,
lips wet,
as you taste of the grape.

Sherri A. Tillman

Archetypal Dreamtime

Silence echoes, shadow mimics
slightest footfall in carved-out corridor.
Ahead, rows left and right;
scores of doors closed
but not locked I know.

Miles they descend,
passages and entryways,
pillared, ornate or spare,
ancient or cuneiformed,
stone-henged.

They breathe a presence.
Each patiently waits.
Arm arcs to turn as
night blind, I stumble in,
a jester in my own dream.

Treasures spill out,
remnants and reason.
Intricate carvings
of wood and wall.
Age faded brocade.

Bronzes patinaed with time.
Urns patterned with
jewels and soot.
Clay pots whose fluid curves
push out in feminine form.

Discarded easels,
work-worn and well-loved.
Ferris wheel seats
and carnival debris,
Scarabs and calliope horses.

Sherri A. Tillman

Archetypal Dreamtime (continued)

A carpet of gold coins cluttered
around tomes of esoteric a
too heavy to lift
but fall open freely
at the slightest glance.

Moved to other access.
Knowing I must go in.
Unfinished images hang
corner to border.
I recognize them all.

I have been led to a cavernous
underground gallery, ancient.
It heralds from eons past,
stuffed with paintings hung.
Lives unknown or realized.

Illuminated by candelabras,
fireflies rhythmical, fluid,
mysterious, entrancing.
It washes over, rendering
a melody macabre.

An opus for the senses.
Humid orchids overgrown,
growing still as I watch.
Twisting imperfect pirouettes of
burnished cord, fossil and word.

A vital tapestry of petal,
life, scent and pain.
Pulsating with flickers of
passionate flame,
fires flight, fecundity.

Archetypal Dreamtime (continued)

Float the underground
channel around a bend
I want to turn back. Please.
But shafts of light pierce darkness
and I am drawn.

Vast calm water opens
caves wide stone mouth.
Channel flows to lagoon,
peace overcomes desire.
I float across blue-green water.

Trailing sated fingers,
I reach the far shore.

Sherri A. Tillman

Wild and Tender Wisdoms

Gently, so gently to heart's beating,
for 'tis a home
where meaning seeks solace.

Breathe in my scent of orchid,
my love, devoured in my gaze.
Give back to me my heart on fire,
set by the hooded embers in your eyes.

Soothe me here then catch me
as I dance a whirling dervish
to cloud-strewn tempests fluid.

Delighted and content,
fiery and impassioned
we come to one another now.

We seek the Mysteries.
A brilliant glowing on verdant paths,
overgrown with providence.

A precious blooming,
does it proffer with
wild and tender wisdoms.

Sherri A. Tillman

Feast of Innocents/ Blessed Be Iago

Each arrives having traveled
an endless expanse of time and will,
gathering bon mots and vessels of wisdom
from paths and drifts of talus along the way.
Markers of stele and imago stand,
plucked from within briars of pain.

Some have stepped
with a measured stride.
Others, with whimper and bellow,
crying in choruses of unease.
Some force-fed. Yet others have searched
Braille-like, urgent and determined.

Each arrives clutching an orb,
guileless in its design. Acquired
by courage or sleight of hand
or by a glimpse of some unknowable grail.
While each sphere pulses,
some do emit a coded radiance.

The banquet set with finest porcelain.
Each stemmed goblet placed
with precision on a table
adorned with the rarest of blossoms.
Silver gleams upon the finest of linen.

Each traveler finds a seat.
Eyes survey and deep sighs follow.
See the opulence spread out.
Realize this is the feast of all feasts.
Observers stand readied to serve.

Sherri A. Tillman

Feast of Innocents/ Blessed Be Iago (continued)

Course by course the meal
is served. Golden salad du jours
of memory, chilled and garnished by
stardust and fresh-ground humor.
Followed by splendid herbed
and savory roasted shanks of life.

Accompanied with luscious bits
of braised ironic delight.
Glazed compotes of fictional science.
Sauces of bittersweet tears.
Mounds of creamy passions so succulent,
liquored by tender salience.

Amidst the raillery and repartee,
with flowing wines
and gullets widened,
Some travelers partake so
deeply, with a great joy.

Others of note decline, preferring
Instead to pick apart the proffered feast.
Focusing on minute detail,
how the parsley doesn't curl graciously
or whether or not the grain of
parody Foi Gras was at its peak.

How the napkins lean off kilter
or what that one dared to wear.
The shank too tough,
the dessert too tart to taste,
the salad is wilted by stars.

Sherri A. Tillman

Feast of Innocents/ Blessed Be Iago (continued)

Such travelers to the feast are starving,
seated at a banquet of infinite love,
unable to take part.
Hungry and wanting.
Resentful and self-exiled.
They rail against communion.

Each brings to the celebration
a single orb, perfect
in it's design. Acquired by
courage or sleight of hand,
indeed. Perhaps Knowing
of the vessel in not enough.

While each sphere pulses,
some emit a fearful shield,
while others radiate brilliance.

C.J. Rider

Sherri A. Tillman

Dialogue with My Inner Medusa

All right. So you've lured me
back here once again.
I came of my own volition,
I suppose you'll say?
Pulled in and taunted by
claustrophobic damned chambers
that mock my return.
Laughing? No, sobbing.

Do you not understand?
Must you insist I stay so near?
Ever inside a feral room,
attached to the umbilicus
you would have me
believe connects us?

Have I not opened enough pulsing
veins, bled mortal rivers?
Screamed and rocked
the self to sleep in the recesses
of this tortured cell?

Caught up in the rage of ancients
who must pass through each painful
wormhole, gasping, clawing.
When will you find your peace?
When will you let me free?
When? WHEN???

So, here I am at your command.
Even as starry nights beckon,
and liquid stirrings, tenuous,
invite of bliss, yet here I linger,
feeding the insipid beast.

Sherri A. Tillman

Dialogue with My Inner Medusa (continued)

Mouthful after mouthful,
Ravenous, and you are never,
NEVER satisfied, never sated.
If I could cut the cord, severed
cleanly, I might. But then?
I would no longer be whole, would I?

Even as I would amputate
my hungry heart,
I know it would re-grow
like a phantom limb
until I give in once again.

What feat of smiling coercion will
you have me commit this time?

Sherri A. Tillman

My Secret Garden

Shall I tell you of
my secret garden?
Found nestled in the
rounded curves
of haunch and mind.
Not many are invited
to the sensual feast.

Where buds of lust,
and joy and seed
bloom and writhe
in a sinuous tandem.

Where veiled thoughts
beget fervent action
and none are lost to
the wayside of an act.

The mind responds as it
sends corporeal signals,
coded pulses to nether regions
in tremulous breathing cadence.
Come, my lover, play.

Bodies, dusted in gold silken pollen,
Delivered on strands of web, wafted
across our union with delicate
imprecision, between
rustlings of the willow's limbs.

Bathed with the crushed emollients
of a noble sacrifice, legions of
petals, clover and stemmed grasses
whose gentle offerings become
a lover's carpet, growing
intoxicating in the heavy loam.

Sherri A. Tillman

My Secret Garden (continued)

Washing out in perfect spiral,
coiled and ready to rise.
Liquid, as the river
running through a
needful response.

The urge a tempered pace,
stroking, parting, tasting,
delicious wandering vines
entwined, attached, you and I.

Sighs unbind the wanting,
two deeply rooted hearts
joined as the trunk of life,
cries out in a reclamation of soul.
Hot with nature's succulent
imperative to merge.

The eyes of wood nymphs,
heavy and hooded,
watch over our garden.
Such desires lie waiting,
precious, on winding paths.

Whose tender footsteps
tempt the toe when traveled.
Where guttural rasps
of earthy musk and rutted scent
beckon the carnal heart.

A lover's creed.
Cries of bliss ring out
so loud and pure
as the undulant forest stirs
within it's slumber.
Ancient garden, this secret one.

Sherri A. Tillman

My Secret Garden (continued)

Each pleasure calls,
shadowed and shameless.
We are ageless angels here,
touched each day
in our places of need.

Caressed we are,
through an emerald canopy
as a tender sun enters,
ethereal, glowing.
To bathe and feed each bloom.
Enter my Secret Garden.

Lush and dense,
ripe and swollen,
your wells and ponds
and pools of spring
providing a sustenance
beyond measure.

Listen to the luminous moon
sing her lyrical song, fluid and trembling.
Dreams to guide the tentative step.
Roses, jasmine, orchids
waft through senses.
Original Delight, come with me to play.

Sensual hide-n-seek in the
bells of Jonquils opened
near velvet-mossed stone
underlining a lover's union.
Reposed in shadow,
in delight, you cry out.

Sherri A. Tillman

My Secret Garden (continued)

Jump, skip and sparkle
each diamond-fleck, glittering.
See how each pebbled specter
dances upon her surface?
Awash with shimmering
secreted quartz?

Watching,
we each learn
the language of
the dragonfly's flight.

Speak, my lover, in tongues
Of heathered frond.
Hang upon
Oak's weathered arm,
swinging, as only
an innocent might.

Grinning, delighted,
oh, mysterious pageant.
Reckless, carefree,
spiritual and wild.
You are here now,
My lover, my twin soul.
Come play with me.

Sherri A. Tillman

Soul Deep ... Time

When one considers
the substance of time,
is it formed in units,
a fine Golden Mean?

Or is it lines graphed,
spiraling ever outward
in parametrical space,
in lush loops of star wind
as it radiates from Source?

Is time held precious,
living in burnished
quicksilver cells
of synapses and ohm?

Perhaps it hides,
residing in polished brass
deflecting and reflecting
the stranger's approach.

Can time be bartered
for attention so fine,
cumquats, rubies or
sweet amber wine?

Is it silken words that salve
the beast, lest time leer,
at once lurid and divine
a certainty, a rose,
God's infinite prose?

Sherri A. Tillman

Soul Deep ... Time (continued)

Can time contract and expand,
plumb the depths of the seas,
arrow deep into space
To circle 'round

Embrace an ellipse imperfect,
to find Neither end nor where it began?
Can time steal grace,
or imprison the mind?

Can time arrive on tiptoe
to savage a bite
from one blissful vision,
to ease one broken heart?

If asked so sweetly would time give back
the already-pulled trigger, the unformed cast?
Take back the guttural cry? Rescind hate's stoic rage?
Will it point the weapon toward the sky
instead of at the extinguished life?

Does time lie down with infinite calm,
replete in the Siren's arms,
breast deep in layers
of gold-leafed palm?

Soul immersed in tradition,
Its history passed along the way,
carrying the cadenced song
arrested in a silver oak
as our ancestors' guard?

Can time be given...
And then withdrawn?

Sherri A. Tillman

To Sculpt A Lover

her pleasure…
dense and silky, darkly veined
alabaster stone retaining heat
freshly quarried find
carved into this image
so well known

she takes up the chisel
in gloves perfectly formed to fit,
in hands that lingered over and loved
the lines that emerge

tools cradled in those skillful hands
knock off all extraneous matter
discovering, uncovering, recovering
the soul of the stone,
of life itself

grinding the rock-flesh
polishing it to a sheen
labor intensive motion
with an arc of sensual pleasure

ancient glowing totem
to tease and guide
to seek and find
the curve 'n line
of hip divine

good lord
call me home

it might need, too
a jagged pounding
a curve
a heated ring

Sherri A. Tillman

To Sculpt A Lover (continued)

spots so embered
with its building fire
the tentative hand
might wince
but never withdraw

oiled and sheened
hard and ready
softly to my mark

I'd use these lover's hands
to form the perfect wordless art
to touch by proxy
he who beckoned this act

C.J. Rider

Lisa Throgmorton

Impassioned Spirits

She stands alone,
Tonight's tale dispassionately unfolds.
The silent ache, frozen in time,
Searches empty horizons.
Insight despairs with an insatiable wanting
As she looks through a crowd of limited eyes.
Longing warmth queries a sea of devoid spirits.
A mist, rare and mystical, unseen,
Treads softly touching none.

Disheartened dreams forfeit fervor's intensity
As reminiscent ardor interrupt and remind
Warming the spirit of familiar hues.
Distrust hauntingly hovers and flees
With a simple nudge of consciousness's glance.
"Is it he?" Whispers enchantment's lure wittily.
Falcon's sears challenge
"Soar beyond what is."

Lifetimes journeying unequaled souls end,
No longer alone.
Complimentary wisdom caresses and satiates
Longing's heated embrace,
While willful patience revels in undressed passions.
Fingertips retrace and design each delicacy of Soul's spirit
As lips indulge in desire's propensity.
Intertwining spirits atone.
Fate recalls
It is us as it always has been.

Lisa Throgmorton

New Beginnings

Unseen potential remains
Safely tucked into nature's womb
As winter threatens with icy fingers,
Touching down its chilled spell.
The earth warms and nestles her child,
Blanketed from the bitter embrace;
Withered flourishings of seasons past,
Preserve imprints of budding beauty.

Several seasons pass over.
Life thunders and flashes its heartbeat,
Rousing tightly wrapped buds and bulbs
Waking, to writhe and flutter with life.
Pushing through, free from creation's tie,
Petals fan out to drink spring's elixir.
Fragrant scents intoxicate with colorful casts
Romancing many, tipsy on its loveliness.

Heaven's tears cleanse, rushing over and in
Unsettling the earth,
Quenching tomorrow's new day
Thirsting to replenish and revive
All the cold season's incantation lulled under.
Overflowing prisms of nature's warmth
Create hope, cosmos's cure to every ailment,
Awakening the new day's blossom with a kiss.

Lisa Throgmorton

Fear Thunders

This terror wakens my sleeping spirit
Your almighty power strikes, crashing down.
Rumbling the earth, its protests ripple out
I wither within; vulnerable, scared
Far away from your gavel's judging sound.

Counting out silence I pray you're far off
Trembling, my heart races doubling its beats.
Craving safety my senses sharpening
Transposing the braille of each lightening strike
Lashing humanity's fallible feats.

Is this a reminder of our frailty
Demonstrating what your swift wrath could bring?
Striking kingdoms to ashes with a flash;
By now this insanity should have paled
But Grandma's words of forewarnings still sting.

Thirty-six years of wisdom and knowledge,
Should her anxieties be placed aside?
The hot and cold air are merely clashing
Brewing a loud display of energy
As tears flow down to cleanse man's foolish pride.

Lisa Throgmorton

Simply Sam

My emotions brim over,
Too much sorrow for just a cat.
Exhausted with this sense of melancholy,
Remembering when he lurked in trees
Some days he'd flat out drop and attack.

I feel foolish getting lost in such sentiment,
As our pet is laid to rest.
Such heartache should be left to the children
Could I say that he was sweet? Unfortunately,
His Siamese antagonism made him a pest.

He'd set up prohibition, lying waiting,
Squirrels disallowed to come down from the trees.
Our little bobcat in cat's clothing,
Sneaking in to castaway on each car outing,
Terrorizing like a pirate on the high seas.

Tufts of silver-gray fur would go flying,
A teen to the elder cat of eighteen years.
We had wondered if we made a mistake getting him
A challenge to our toddler, his nemesis
A child, leaving Sam trembling, hiding in fear.

Stalking the neighborhood chicken,
Her chicks would cross over his open paw.
We could almost see his tongue hanging out
As he lie sideways, savoring saliva dripping,
A delicious, chick treat to fill his retracting claw.

Beautiful like a child when sleeping,
Stretching out in the charm he brought to this place,
He was simply my Sam, silky, snow-down softness
Rolling around in and shredding exotic plants
His memory I can't seem to erase.

Lisa Throgmorton

Simply Sam (continued)

He had everyone in the house seething,
Grumbling, sometimes wishing he'd go away.
Those beautiful ocean eyes, tail twitching,
Contemplating who he'd toy with next
Claws extended, he just wanted to play.

The summer day seemed quietly empty,
We looked all over the place, not a sound,
From our mischievous ball of feisty fur
Searching favorite spots on the property
Our Sam could not be found.

The neighbor's eyes held sadness
As she approached, walking my way.
Not knowing how to tell me
I'm so sorry, I think I found something that's yours
Under the blossoming cherry tree he lay.

The most painful thing about losing him,
Only being in our lives for but a year,
Is thinking the thoughts of the unknown
Did he suffer, how did he die?
Missing those last moments, I shed a tear.

Lisa Throgmorton

Chance's Child

A child of chance dressed in humility
Kept dispirited eyes to the ground.
Wearing tattered clothes and straggly hair,
Her Mum lost to a fevered bed,
She stretched out her tin for charity
Ailing hope implored even a pound.

Pity coined from gifting hands
Not one soul paused to think twice.
"Surely this will buy some elixir,
A crumb or two to quiet empty growls."
When night came calling, it found
Each consciousness redeemed at a price.

Then one with a vain chill came boasting by
That warmth she could not resist.
"Child, you should be sorely shamed
Making a spectacle of yourself,
How could your mum allow such behavior?
Your likes has no right to exist."

"Protocol you couldn't even spell,
You're a mere contagion to society.
Why not do us all a favor?
Return to your mother, inept one,
Escort her to that middle ground,
Join her and say goodbye for me."

A dank chill wrapped her in her smug bitterness,
Her heartless words would resound no more.
This lady of self-serving high society
Fear radiated up and down her spine
Tripping on relentless egotism
Finding herself at her bitter-wishes' door.
Across the street her own mother stepped,

Lisa Throgmorton

Chance's Child (continued)

Unaware, into a flowing tear-drenched street.
Life poured out fate her daughter had created
Self-centered spoken words ricocheted
Its swift arrow, a horse drawn carriage
Raced out of control towards inevitability.

That moment delivered intent without a word
Mouth gaping, her heart fell to the ground.
What had she done to deserve this?
The loss of being abandoned without her mum felt,
Years of condescending air suffocating
This day no superiority could be found.

The metal of tin clanked as it fell to the earth
The child dashed, grabbing the woman's hand, yanking fast.
Running towards death's destination, screams shrilled
Behind hooves raised, protesting heart's hammered out
A soul softening as arms held mum and chance's child
Safe from harm, on the sidewalk spilled redemption cast.

Lisa Throgmorton

Reaching out

Where does the mere mortal look
When seeking heightened advice?
Sitting on perceptive instincts
Masking Mars of the professional,
The shield's illusion falters at a price.

Why let another direct one's strategies?
Demigods, too, struggle with their life.
Plagued by flaws and temptations,
The heavens they tread tremble
As they indulge themselves in strife.

Where is the hope for the seekers
Reaching out for help, grasping the edge,
Shaking as the mind sees the hypocrisy,
Battled insecurities, question knowledge?
The warrior loses his grip on sanity's ledge.

Is there a certificate of proficiency
For those who dangle the quick-fix key,
Implying the embodiment of perfection?
A myth? Answers lie not in another
Nor found extraneously.

Solutions sought, resonate closely,
Tucked deep within our soul's inner-self.
We've been granted the aptitude,
A healing of sorts, drawing from our gifts
Hidden wisdoms, treasures for us to delve.

Lisa Throgmorton

Reaching out (continued)

However, the mythos overcomes with conquest
When lost, a compass, guiding our way.
Sometimes there's that individual to drive us
Stretching us beyond our limitations
When denial can no longer be the stay.

We must take care in our explorations
When sacrificing our vulnerable self.
Accreditation doesn't deem absoluteness,
But hope's chance for scaling nothingness
When the empty well's left nothing else.

Lisa Throgmorton

Love' Last Promise

Misfortune cast its spell
Filling me with loneliness,
Tasting life's poison apple.
Trembling, I dread the numbness
Of being on the outside alone.
Looking in, beyond the windows,
My family continues on
Embracing enchantment's warmth,
As if I never was.

Drowning in sorrow
Tattered dreams wither
In the dark dungeons.
Abandoned, an ache
Floods me with despair
As memories of
Our "Happily Ever After"
Shatter like a broken mirror
Into the nothingness that's mine.

You gifted me fleeting love,
Never mine to embrace.
My prince regressed to that of a beast
Imprisoning me with contempt's curse,
As love's bud wilts.
I pay the price
As I watch another
Steal away the glass slipper
Lusting over that which we created.

Lisa Throgmorton

Love' Last Promise (continued)

Fairy fate lends deaf ears on
My silent cries that echo into eternity
Pleading for understanding
A decade and a half of denial
That sweet lips once
Stirred the soul's wake.

Life turns its page on my troubles.
Each day unfolding new blossoms,
Granting me life's jewels, new beginnings
Richer for your absence
Yet amiss you stole my fairytale
For I have lost faith in love's kiss.

Nora D. Watterson

First Night Home

As you drift off to slumber land,
I wonder at Gods' plan.
My hand does drift to touch your brow,
Immersed in why's and how.
Your face bathed in fading twilight,
Fills me with awed delight.

New to me the feelings rendered
Pride, joy, love are tendered.
I gaze upon your body small
Smiling, I have it all.
Grasping my finger in your sleep
Tears well, I almost weep.

Praying that I perchance bestow
All your needs as you grow
For just a mouth to be stuffing
Finished equals nothing
But to instill beauty of soul
This should be greatest goal.

I know not what tomorrow brings,
My voice now softly sings.
A melody unique as time,
Mothers' love weaves the rhyme.
We're here at last, our first night home,
Sentry post till you're grown.

Nora D. Watterson

The Prowler

The tapping of the sleeting rain,
Rouses her from slumber.
Wind whistling round the windowpane,
Sounds of distant thunder.
Sleeping baby beneath her breast,
Within the cozy king-sized bed.
Nagging, a feeling of unrest,
She slowly raises up her head.

The tapping seems all too insistent,
Under the shade, beneath the curtain.
Tentatively, she crosses the distance,
Sounds of which she must be certain.

Formidable specter, behind the panes,
His tool attempts to force the latch.
Adrenalin, blood frigid smites her veins,
She's lost, alone, her breath does catch.
Fear rises in hurricane proportions,
Threatening to set her adrift.
The mind races thru it's own contortions,
Reasoning on a downward shift.

To remove the babe where he lies sleeping,
The greatest care is taken.
She places him in brother's keeping,
Her prayer's they won't awaken.

Door is silently closed, then locked,
She gropes upon the closet shelf.
Blindly searching for bullets stocked,
Not one indulgence for herself.
Heart of a lioness starts to roar,
Senses heightened, her cubs at stake.
The cloud of rage billows, free to soar,
For him, she waits, on fury's gate.

Nora D. Watterson

The Dreaming

A photo framed beneath the glass,
She sits within the rocking chair.
Dark eyes that follow when I pass,
As white as snow, well-groomed her hair.
My brother placed upon her lap,
Sailor suit with buttons gleaming.
I almost hear how feet would tap,
It carries me to the dreaming…

Two weeks to spend at grandma's house,
Sun drenched days in happy splendor.
Awake and button up your blouse,
Cajole and whine till she'd surrender.
It's off to cousin's you must go,
To play among the daffodils.
Bright sunlight streams, a breeze does blow,
She waits for you on windowsill.

The race is on, off to the stables,
Glimpses of a newborn colt in hay.
Up the ladder, on to the gables,
A tea party at large, you now play.
Under the rafters, having a ball,
At role playing, you are quite heady.
From the doorway your aunt does call,
"It's time to eat, the lunch is ready."

A storm rolls in while you are seated,
Thunder booms, shivering down your spine.
On this day, you won't be defeated
One game of choice, seeming divine.
You're dreaming of your uncle's house,
Scampering up narrow back stairway.
Playing hide and seek, quiet as a mouse,
Not seeing what will block your airway.

Nora D. Watterson

The Dreaming (continued)

Shadows deepen in late afternoon
Many rooms, massive and confusing.
Silence poignant, a dust ridden gloom,
Fact, you're lost, not slightly amusing.
You hear your grandma calling your name,
Which direction should you turn or go?
Gas lights they flicker, ignite with flame,
Down the corridor your legs do flow.

Finally, you reach the marble stairs,
Go past sweet flowers in a basket.
Three steps down, she rises up and glares,
For you have stepped, into her casket.
It wracks your bones, chilling the marrow,
Pieces of your heart's demolition.
Not once to play at cards of tarot
You, who have witnessed premonition.

The photo I could not abide,
Yet a child, just turned eleven.
A guilt I kept locked deep inside,
Not understanding earth or heaven.
She sits within the rocking chair,
So great the love It knew no bounds.
Beautiful eyes and snow white hair,
I feel her always, still around.

Nora D. Watterson

Etchings in the Glass

Facets of the solitaire
Brilliant neath the hot white glare.

Emotions reel and pirouette.
Playing often at coquette.

Within the windows of the mind.
Traces of the ball of twine.

Love, happiness, pain and suffering.
The soul tested to do its buffering.

Belief in God, or agnostic.
Eternal hope, flipside caustic.

Thoughts that stray and run amok.
Things we do and wish for luck.

Passage of time not always luminous.
Remembrance placed upon the humorous.

As humans we seem ever driven.
To challenge what to whom is given.

Paths are chosen, journeys traveled.
Best laid plans come unraveled.

Choices in life leave a residual.
Upon the face of each individual.

Visions in the looking glass.
Often empty, sometimes crass.

So be careful while you're sketching.
What in time you may be etching.

Nora D. Watterson

I Speak To You

I talk to you, your ears are always closed.
Yet, mine should be open when you whisper.
I search my soul, endlessly seeking, what???
Peace eludes, darkness cloaks my inner self.
Thoughts of how I knew you, better than most
Mundane, they fall short, on loves' empty ghost.

It seems you were not all I imagined,
Picket fences torn, remain uprooted.
A desert of despair revolves shifting.
Blinding my eyes, ripping my entire soul.
I possess not, the pill to cure my ills,
Creeping, like mold, upon vast windowsills.

The line runs thin, taut, betwixt love and hate
Taste of fruit that's bittersweet with resin
It coats my soul in runoff trapped inside
Pockmarked, gouged, festering boil of turmoil
Lancing takes tremendous strength, fortitude
Abandoned, told I have an attitude.

You transform before my eyes, not seeing
Elixir of booze destroys earned respect.
Overpowering wedlock once offered,
I hold no regrets about refusal.
Path traveled before in my lifetime,
Where love evolves, a chore of the nighttime.

"I speak to you, muted it falls on deaf ears"

Eye Candy

Biographies – Introducing the Authors

Dr. Karina J. Belkin
Dr. Karina Jaide Belkin was born in the Former Soviet Union in 1971. She is now living in New York with her husband and two children. She holds a bachelor's, master's and doctorate degree in naturopathy and is currently finishing a dissertation for her second doctorate degree in the philosophy of natural healing. Alternative medicine and hypnosis are her areas of work. Besides her family and career, most of her time is spent studying the middle path of righteousness and the teachings of the Ascended Masters. She is a student of the light and of life. A fourteen year vegetarian/ vegan, she holds all life streams dear. Her passions include her children, reading, writing, singing, gourmet cooking, yoga, higher spirituality and spreading light and love to all those in need.

Elric Bowdean
Elric is forty going on fifteen, born and raised in California and still waiting to see the world. He's married to a lovely lady Cindy and they have two wonderful daughters Amber and Crystal. Finally after all these years he feels he's getting to know who he is. "I love life, the beach, mountains and I hate the snow. Love has always been a struggle for me so I guess this is why a lot of my poems have a dark side to them. I have picked up the pen again and begun pouring out my soul for all to see. It has been over 20 years since I lasted penned a poem. Today I have found the reason to start writing. Thank you Terry."

Michael Cotner
Michael R. Cotner has been writing poems on and off for some twenty-eight years now. This love-hate relationship began as high school freshman, when he was encouraged by a caring English teacher to enter a Scholastic Magazine writing contest. He was awarded sixth place out of five thousand entries. Almost three decades later he finds himself unable to put down his quill for more than a few months at a time. It has become his life's goal to someday write one of histories greatest love poems. Until that time he finds his

Michael Cotner (continued)
muse where he can, having just purchased a modest five bedroom farm house in the middle of the Illinois countryside, he hopes to find new vistas to write about. Michael is inspired by his loving wife and four children and hopes one of them may be encouraged to follow in his footsteps. Michael Cotner is also one of the co-authors/co-producers of the first *Tapestries of the Heart*.

Timothy Michael Flaherty
Timothy lives in Western Maryland with his wife and 4 of his 8 children. He has been writing since he was a young boy. "My father always encouraged my writing. I have been published in several ezines including Poetry Repairs and Storyteller Web Magazine. This is my first hard cover publication and I am pleased to be included with such talented poets."

James M. Furber
As a youth, Furber wrote hundreds of poems and tossed them in the trash. It wasn't until he had the good fortune to meet the love of his life, Theresa, that he became more confident in his abilities. She became his wife and inspiration. She encouraged him to explore his poetic talents and to stop throwing his poems away! Furber states: "Theresa is the left side of my heart and we go together well." His life experiences have offered him much material to draw upon for his writing. He is an accountant by trade and currently manages financial affairs for several small companies. Along with fatherhood, he has managed to be a community volunteer. For over twenty years Furber has worked with young boys as a mentor, baseball coach, director and professional baseball scout. Furber always loved poetry and has now decided to pursue that love in an innovative way. He is the founder of a poetry-based website, "EmergingPoets.com." He also created the book *Tapestries of the Heart* and expects it will become an annual publication. Since meeting Theresa, he has written and saved, many poems. Some of these, he has generously included in the initial volume of *Tapestries of the Heart*.

James Hastings
James A. Hastings, born in Brownsville, Texas in 1954 has been writing poetry since his college days in the early 1970's. With a love for life and nature, Jim's poems reflect those desires in both free-verse and rhyme. Jim is married and has three teen-aged daughters. He currently resides in western Kentucky and works as a Surgical Technologist in Nashville, Tennessee. James is also co author/co producer of the very first *Tapestries of the Heart*.

Hannah Hastings
Hannah is a seventeen year old, home schooled student that has been writing ever since she was eight years old. Hannah is planning to go into law enforcement and is currently a member of Law Enforcement Explorer Post 111. When she is not writing, Hannah enjoys reading, drawing, and spending time with her family.

Robert Lock
Bob Lock was born in Gower, near Swansea, Wales in 1949. The same city in which Dylan Thomas (his favorite poet) was born and bred. He has an Italian wife, two children and one grandson. After leaving school he started working for a brewery as a clerk, after twenty-five years with the same company and attaining the position of Engineer he decided to expand his horizons and moved to Italy for four years. There he taught English in a number of private schools and finally became a translator for a large foundry that had ties with British Steel. Now, having taken early retirement, he passes his time writing short stories and poems. Some of which have been published, but the elusive novel publication has still eluded him, but for how long?

Mark Manis
Mark Manis, has been writing poetry off and on since 1981. He graduated from Morehead State University in 1990 with a Bachelors Degree in History and Radio/Television. He later went back in 1998 and received his Masters Degree in Special Education. Mark likes to write on a different variety of subjects that span from nature, to observations he's witnessed in life. Mark currently works as a special

education teacher in Northern Kentucky with his wife Becky, and his two cats.

James Oldfield
James is a twenty-year-old English and Philosophy student from Manchester, England. He has been writing since his early teens, but only within the last year has it become a serious past-time. Where once poetry was a mere vent for angst, now it is a passion, and he rarely feels complete without some poem or plot idea for him to play around with. Generally he favors the more traditional forms of poetry with distinct rhyme and meter, but he is also prone to experiment, and is always willing to try a new style. He draws most of his inspiration from people, rather than things, and is particularly interested in reflecting on human nature as he currently sees it.

Alexander Pavelich
Alexander Pavelich is a fifteen-year-old student with an extreme appetite for writing poetry and stories. He was born in the United States, but moved to Norway at the age of one and is living there currently. Alex first began writing at the age of ten and always writes whenever there is time. His urge for writing will probably keep going, and perhaps he is sitting at his desk, writing right now.

Cynthia Jeanne Rider
Cynthia Jeanne Rider was born in Sandusky Ohio. At an early age, she was introduced to the arts by her grandfather who deeply impressed her by accurately drawing a deer from memory and making up a short flowing story to go with it. From that day forward Cynthia has been involved in many artistic endeavors that include various media and technique. In 1993, Cynthia Rider received her degree in Arts. She is currently an educator, artist, musician, and poet. She has also taught music and art and has a working knowledge of computer graphics and web design. As an accomplished artist, Ms. Rider now writes melodious verse, fusing romantic and earthly elements to compliment her artwork and photography.

Lorraine R. Sautner
Lorraine R. Sautner is a lifelong New England resident living in Fairfield County, Connecticut. She has always appreciated the beauty of the written word and experienced her first brush with local writing success in 1976 with her winning essay about the Bicentennial. Lorraine graduated with a BA degree in English/Writing from Western Connecticut State University, where she served as a Reporter, Associate Editor and Copy Editor of the school's newspaper, *The Echo*. She worked for many years in the newsroom of the Danbury News-Times and is currently employed in the executive recruitment field in Stamford, Connecticut. She is currently pursuing a graduate degree in Library and Information Science at The Pratt Institute in New York City. Lorraine enjoys writing poetry with spiritual and transcendental themes and views her writing as a vehicle for sharing her faith in Jesus Christ.

Jennifer Penix-Taylor
Jennifer Penix-Taylor is a 27-year-old college student who is working on her bachelor's degree in criminal psychology. She's had aspirations to be a writer since she was a child. However, while in her teens lost the inspiration to write. Creative writing class in college has piqued her interest once again. Her husband and their eight-year-old daughter encouraged her to write once again. Jennifer writes like she reads, some days her mood takes her to explore love, on others horror, and then some days she will write epic tales about warriors of old. She lives in comfort in Southern Ohio with her daughter Kennedy and husband Robert.

Sherri A. Tillman
Ms Tillman has worn many metaphorical hats in her lifetime. Mother of one son first and foremost, painter and sculptor, educator, jazz singer, social critic, and constant seeker of an indefinable divinity to peak from the most mundane of happenstance. She, being the eldest of 4 children, is imbued with a spirit of independence, well honed with a touch of Sixties defiance that has placed itself securely within her mindset. Having mellowed with the natural course of time it is her curious nature that has brought her to be the shaper of the words she writes and the images she paints. Born in South Carolina and having

relocated to the Midwest early in her years, her family settled in St. Louis, Missouri where Ms Tillman still resides. She attended prestigious Font Bonne College in St. Louis, where she received her degrees in Studio Art having studied painting under the exquisite tutelage of master painter, Victor Wang. She has operated an art studio for many years and her art has shown in many of the galleries in the city. She currently teaches art to urban city children. A city dweller, Ms Tillman was one of the co-founders of a group of poets to organize and become known as the Soulard Culture Squad. She has volunteered her time and energies to assist the elderly within the community and continues to be of service where and when she can.

Lisa Throgmorton
Lisa is a married, mother of four children. She can be found nestled in the foothills of Northern California. Her interests include writing, reading, cycling and anything that draws her closer to nature. She aspires to eventually complete her teaching credential, in hopes some day she will work as a Jr. High guidance counselor with our most valuable resource we can invest time into, our children.

Nora D. Watterson
Born and raised in the heart of the Midwest, she was the third of four children. Her childhood was spent growing up in the middle of three rambunctious brothers. She attended public school until her freshman year, when she was enrolled in a private Christian academy. Always possessing a wild free spirit, she never completed high school. August of 1979 brought the birth of her first child. Years following brought marriage, divorce, and four additional children. The lack of education forced her into the food service industry. Working sixty plus hours weekly, she has been a waitress for over twenty years. The cost of a wayward spirit has been high and is reflected in some of her poems. In 1999 she moved to Seattle, Washington. She now resides in a suburb on the outskirts, enjoying the views of the mountains and surrounding countryside. The youngest of her five children resides with her and is her greatest source of joy and support.

About the Author

Three poets, each a stranger, had the same dream. Frustrated with phoney promises of having their works published that lead nowhere, they envisioned a book where new poets like themselves would not only be recognized but actually be compensated for their efforts.

Through the Internet, James Furber, Michael Cotner, and James Hastings met and shared their dream with each other. Was it possible to actually publish a book of poetry featuring unknowns who had nothing but great talent and the dream to see it through? These three men thought that it was.

With a release date of December 2003, "Tapestries of the Heart—Emerging Poets of the 21st Century" will be the culmination of this mutual dream

Printed in the United States
1544900002BA/224